WHERE DO I GO FROM HERE?

ESTHER DRILL

HEATHER MCDONALD

REBECCA ODES

WITH LOUISA KAMPS

W9-AOM-199

PENGUIN BOOKS

PENGUIN BOOKS
Published by the Penguin Group
Penguin Putnam Inc.
375 Hudson Street
New York, NY, 10014, U.S.A.
Penguin Books Ltd
7 Wrights Lane
London W8 5TZ, England
Penguin Books Australia Ltd
Ringwood, Victoria, Australia
Penguin Books Canada Ltd
10 Alcorn Avenue
Toronto, Ontario, Canada M4V 3B2
Penguin Books (N.Z.) Ltd
182-190 Wairau Road,
Auckland 10, New Zealand
Penguin Books Ltd, Registered Offices:
Harmondsworth, Middlesex, England

10 9 8 7 6 5 4 3

(c) 2004 iVillage Inc.

All rights reserved, including the right to reproduce
this book or portions thereof in any form whatsoever.
For information, address Penguin Putnam,
375 Hudson Street, New York, NY 10014

CIP data available ISBN 0-14-200214-3

A ROUNDTABLE PRESS BOOK
Roundtable Press, Inc.
Directors: **Julie Merberg** and **Marsha Melnick**
Design: **pink design, inc.** (www.pinkdesigninc.com)
Writing and research: **Louisa Kamps**
Editor: **Sara Newberry**
Production editor: **John Glenn**
Editorial assistant: **Caitlin Earley**

THANKS!

First and foremost, thanks to everyone at Roundtable Press for shepherding this book from concept to finished product. Special thanks go out to Roundtable regulars Julie Merberg, Sara Newberry, Caitlin Earley, top-flight designer Georgia Rucker and ace writer Louisa Kamps.

Special shoutout of gratitude to the members of the gURL community for their contributions and insights into life after high school.

And a sincere, collective thank you to all the people who have helped us on our own paths from life after high school to the present day—including and especially our parents, partners, progeny, and pets. You know who you are.

We love you!!!

table of contents

This book is designed to help you consider the many opportunities available to you as you transition from high school to the world beyond. It can help you learn more about yourself and your immediate goals, and give you some idea of what you might need to do to achieve them. It provides general information (and personal perspectives) on a wide range of post-graduate possibilities, as well as decision-making and other factors you may need to think about as you move toward the next phase of your life. This book is not a comprehensive college guide. It is meant as a companion to the many more detailed reference books you can (and probably should) consult once you have some idea of the direction you'd like to pursue. We provide a list of resources at the end of each chapter to guide you to more specific information that may help you on your path.

introduction

What do you want to be when you grow up?

This is a question most of us have been asked since we can remember. And even though our childhood responses may seem silly now, the question can linger in our minds long after we've "grown up."

Well, our experience is that life doesn't really work that way. You don't "grow up" and "become" something. You evolve into an adult version of yourself, sometimes taking circuitous routes, with unexpected stops along the way.

For most people, life before high school involves

Try to get jobs in New York

Instead apply to graduate school

Work in Silicon Valley at a video game company

Discover the internet while on the job!

Fall in love with NYC while there on extended business trip

Work many part-time jobs

Move to Boston...get a job as a faculty assistant at Harvard University

Go on tour with Love Child as tour manager

Band breaks up

Get job as decorative painter/studio assistant

Try to transfer out. Instead do one year abroad in Belgium

Move to San Francisco two days after graduation

Get laid off from bookstore

Tour US and Europe

Back to college... Russian Studies major

University of Iowa History and Film Major

Year off from college...work at College Hill Bookstore

Graduate... still working at bookstore

Go to graduate school for painting in Chicago

High School in the midwest

Heather's Path

Esther's Path

Quit graduate school to pursue rock stardom

Learn to play bass guitar Start playing in a punk/pop band called Love Child

West Orange High School

Brown University Math major

Rebecca's Path

West Orange High School

Graduate early Go to work at a super-indie music magazine in Boston

Vassar College Art Major

a limited amount of major, life-changing decisions. Of course there are important choices to contend with, but they usually happen within a fairly closed scope of possibilities: whatever classes are available at your school, and whatever extracurricular activities you have interest in and access to. Though it's certainly possible to reach beyond the narrow walls of the typical high school experience, branching out is the exception rather than the rule. For most of us, it's life after high school that presents our first encounter with looming, life-altering life-direction choices. Or so it seems, anyway.

If there's one major message we'd like to communicate in this book, it's that these choices don't have to be as scary as they seem. The reason for this is simple: life paths are not usually straightforward. Just as often as not, they tend to involve some twists and turns, curving sharply to the left when you might have been expecting a straight shot to the finish line. Which means you can feel a little bit freer, when deciding what to do with your life, to stop thinking about every single decision as one that will dramatically and inalterably change your life's course. Each choice makes an impact, true. But there are few roads you might choose where there's no possibility of turning back (or right, left, or diagonally). Life is a journey. Each path we take leads us to different experiences, and we can hopefully learn from those experiences to see if we want to continue full steam ahead on the path we've chosen, or turn in a new direction.

As you can see, our own paths have been far from straightforward. And although we've enjoyed many of the stops we've made along the way, we know that we've got lots more to accomplish and more winding roads to travel (if we're lucky!) We hope you get to travel down your own unique paths, exploring your interests and pursuing your goals. This is a perfect time to start seriously thinking about the world of possibility that awaits you.

So...use this opportunity to find out more about who you are, what matters to you, and where you might want to go from here.

Go to NYU's Interactive Telecommunications Program

Go to NYU's Interactive Telecommunications Program

DEAL WITH IT!

WHERE DO I GO FROM HERE?

Go to NYU's Interactive Telecommunications Program

THE LOOKS BOOK

gURL is born!

Learn how to use computer design programs after hours at the office

Work as design assistant for Christmas tree bow manufacturer

PART 1

EXPLORATION

Nearing the end of high school can feel like looking out of a tunnel into the whole wide world. Sometimes it's easy (maybe even too easy?) to see the huge range of options available to you, and the problem is picking the one that's right for you. Sometimes there's an obvious choice sitting right in front of you, but you're not sure whether it's the step you really want to take. Other times, the whole idea of making a life choice is too scary even to contemplate, and it's tempting just to do whatever's easiest, even if that's not the most gratifying path for you.

Many people pursue some kind of formal education or enter the workforce full-time as soon as they graduate high school. There are infinite possibilities within both of these categories, from four-year colleges to specialty schools where you can learn a specific trade; from temporary internships to jobs that set you on a career path for years. Some students choose to take time to travel, alone or with a group, after graduation.

Making a good decision about what's next means taking a good look at your interests, your goals, and the circumstances of your life. Factoring in both your dreams and your reality (and keeping in mind that this first choice won't necessarily dictate the entire course of the rest of your life) will help you figure out how you might want to spend your time in the near future. Whichever path looks right to you, it's important to remember that every path you consciously choose to pursue at this time in your life can be seen as a legitimate part of your "education."

Four years of college may be the traditional view of higher education, but the reality is that life itself is an education, and there is a world of options to consider when thinking about how you'd like to start your own adult learning process.

Beginning to explore the many available life paths can be inspiring, reaffirming, and sometimes intimidating. It can also give you a chance to look inward and figure out more about who you are and what you like, don't like, are good at, are bored by . . . You may think of yourself as someone who has always known your ideal direction, whether it's the career you've fantasized about since childhood or the college everyone in your family has attended for generations. But regardless of how set you think you are in your plans, it can be helpful, and even eye-opening, to check out what else is out there. You may find that when you really think about the things you enjoy or feel passionate about, or when you envision the life you want for yourself, your priorities shift slightly. Or you may focus in with greater intensity on the path you've planned, knowing for sure it's the one you want to follow (at least for now).

If you make the effort to take a good look at your own life goals and explore the different ways you might achieve them, you'll know that you made the best effort possible to consciously choose the direction of your life. And it's always good to know you are where you are because you wanted to be there, not because it's just where you ended up.

CHAPTER 1.

finding focus

Making a decision about what to do after high school is not about devising one ultimate plan that you must follow from here on out. There can be a lot of pressure from parents, teachers, and even friends for you to figure out what to do with your life before you leave high school. But it's important to give yourself a chance to explore all the options that intrigue you and to remember that career planning usually doesn't happen overnight. Many college students still haven't decided what they're going to major in by sophomore year. And many "successful" adults make major career changes several times in their lives (five, on average), or spend years zigzagging from one job to another before they're happy in a career. Often, the thing you most want to do changes as you evolve and your circumstances shift.

However your own path progresses, developing a strong sense of your unique preferences, values, and talents and gathering information about a wide range of possible career choices will help you start making decisions with confidence and clarity. You'll open your eyes to interesting, unexpected possibilities you never even knew existed. And the idea of moving forward into the future will become a lot less scary and a lot more exciting, since the path you choose—direct, rambling, or anywhere in between—will ultimately help you become more of who you are as an individual. The point is to find out what you're good at, and what makes you happy.

Take a close look at your own temperament, talents, interests, and dreams with these questions.

ask yourself

>> **What activities do you most enjoy or look forward to doing?**

>> What feels easy and natural for you to be doing?

>> **Is there anything you do because you have to do it, or think you should be doing it, when you would rather be doing other things?**

>> Where do you most enjoy being?

>> **Whom do you enjoy being with? (Family, friends, yourself . . .)**

>> Imagine yourself a year from now: Where are you? How does that make you feel in your gut?

>> **How ambitious are you? Are you someone who's more or less content to go with the flow, or are you the kind of person who's always driven to change the status quo?**

>> Can you conjure up an image of yourself doing something in the future—working, studying, or maybe exploring the world—that makes you proud? What would it take to get yourself there?

I made a tough decision between college and singing, but singing is what I love to do. It makes me happy, and lets me express how I feel. I went to NYC to pursue a singing career. Since then, a producer has picked me up because he loves my voice, and we are working to create a great demo to submit to record labels. I have performed in front of huge audiences, and gained a lot of self-confidence. I am very busy, though, and I miss my boyfriend back home so much.

Discover What Makes You Tick

For many people, the idea of leaving the familiar, structured environment of high school is fairly terrifying. Trying to decide what you're going to do after graduation, when there are literally thousands of options, can be overwhelming. Fear of the future tends to come with any major life transition, at any age. One of the best ways to gain control of your fears is to try to get to know yourself a little better. By doing some serious soul-searching now, figuring out what you're good at and which activities give you the most pleasure, you'll find it easier to focus your goals and begin exploring ways to pursue them.

To learn more about yourself and what you might like to do with your life, you can also take something known as a personality test. The famous Swiss psychologist Carl Jung devised a theory that people tend to fit into two key personality types: extroverted (outward-looking) or introverted (inward-looking). Jung also proposed that, beyond extroversion and introversion, people can be categorized according to how they generally function in the world—whether they tend to process things through sensing or through intuition, and whether they tend to evaluate by thinking or by feeling. Obviously, categorizations of people can never fully capture their complex natures and must be taken with a grain of salt.

Operating on the principle that activities and careers that let people express their personalities will give them the most satisfaction, career counselors often use tests based on Jung's "personality theory" to help adults and college students in their search for meaningful work. Typically, guidance counselors don't offer personality tests to teenagers, since high schoolers' temperaments and tastes are often still emerging. But bearing this caveat in mind, you may want to check out some of the fun, potentially thought-provoking personality tests available in career development books and on a number of websites.

FOR CAREER GUIDES AND WEB SITES, SEE P. 17.

THE MYERS-BRIGGS TYPE INDICATOR

One of the most famous personality tests is the Myers-Briggs Type Indicator (MBTI), which is based on Jung's theory of personality types. It measures four key traits:

1. how we interact with the world (our relative levels of extroversion or introversion)

2. what kind of information, tangible or hypothetical, we naturally notice (through sensing or intuition)

3. how we make decisions through thinking or feeling

4. how we prefer to live in the world—by judging it in a structured way, or by perceiving it in a spontaneous way.

Depending on where the MBTI says you stand on each of the four spectra above, you'll be assigned one of sixteen different letter-coded personality types, which can give you a better understanding of your unique way of communicating and inter-acting with others. For example, in the Myers-Briggs system, INFJs—people who tend to be introverted, intuitive (N stands for intuition), feeling, and judging—are thought to be (among other things) careful, compassionate decision makers. And ENTPs—extroverted, intu-itive, thinking, and perceiving people—are enterprising, opti-mistic, outspoken folks.

The Myers-Briggs system is too complicated to go into too much detail here. For more information on how the Myers-Briggs can help put you on a career path, see p. 17.

HOW I GOT HERE

I know that my parents read a lot to me when I was in the womb and I always loved books. I wrote poetry when I was very little. I was encouraged because my mom wrote down a lot of what I said and made me feel that it was valuable. I've written for as long as I can remember. In high school, I wrote poetry and some short-short stories, and became more serious about my desire to be a published author. The character of Weetzie originated at that time and many of her adventures were inspired by that time of my life. Then I started writing short stories and eventually novels. Fiction moved me so much, took me out of myself, connected me to the world . . .

I always write about what excites me, even if I don't think it will interest anyone else. It feels a bit like dreaming, just going deep into your own world.

FRANCESCA LIA BLOCK, AUTHOR

HOW I GOT HERE

For a couple of years I was a senator for my [high school] class. My parents didn't encourage any extracurricular activities that they considered frivolous. So I couldn't go to football games or pep rallies. But if I was at the library or at work—I used to scoop ice cream—that was fine.

My first two years [in college] I was pre-med, because I thought I wanted to be a dentist. About midway through college I decided I really enjoyed business, so I switched to economics and finance. I was an invest-ment banker for about fourteen years. In my spare time, I organized math and science programs in my old junior high school in Anaheim, California.

I went to talk to my congressman about expanding the program and when I didn't get any response, I came home that night and said, "I'm going to run for Congress." I ended up winning my seat by 984 votes.

LORETTA SANCHEZ, CONGRESSWOMAN

THE RISO-HUDSON ENNEAGRAM TYPE INDICATOR

Another test based on Jung's theory of personality that might help you see yourself a little more clearly is the Enneagram. According to the Enneagram Institute, which offers a free version of the RHETI test online, the test—a series of questions designed to gauge your temperament and general style of operating in the world—will tell you which of the following nine types best describes you:

1. **The Reformer** The Rational, Idealistic Type: Principled, Purposeful, Self-Controlled, and Perfectionistic

2. **The Helper** The Caring, Interpersonal Type: Generous, Demonstrative, People-Pleasing, and Possessive

3. **The Achiever** The Success-Oriented, Pragmatic Type: Adaptable, Excelling, Driven, and Image-Conscious

4. **The Individualist** The Sensitive, Withdrawn Type: Expressive, Dramatic, Self-Absorbed, and Temperamental

5. **The Investigator** The Intense, Cerebral Type: Perceptive, Innovative, Secretive, and Isolated

6. **The Loyalist** The Committed, Security-Oriented Type: Engaging, Responsible, Anxious, and Suspicious

7. **The Enthusiast** The Busy, Fun-Loving Type: Spontaneous, Versatile, Acquisitive, and Scattered

8. **The Challenger** The Powerful, Dominating Type: Self-Confident, Decisive, Willful, and Confrontational

9. **The Peacemaker** The Easygoing, Self-Effacing Type: Receptive, Reassuring, Agreeable, and Complacent

To take the complete RHETI test online, go to www.enneagraminstitute.com

DISCOVER YOUR AYURVEDIC PERSONALITY TYPE

For a non-Western perspective on personality, you can look to the ancient Indian self-discovery system known as Ayurveda (essentially, the "knowledge" or "science" of life in Sanskrit). According to Ayurvedic principles, a healthy mind and body can be maintained by keeping a balance of five elements—earth, fire, water, air, and ether—in the body. Ayurveda categorizes people into personality types called "doshas." The three basic doshas are Vata, Pitta, and Kapha, and each is a combination of two elements which are associated with unique mental and emotional qualities. Though many people share characteristics of two or sometimes all three dosha types, although it is believed that most people have a dominant dosha. The nature of the doshas, and the potential pitfalls of each personality, are:

Vata, a mix of air and fire, tend to be enthusiastic, creative people when they're in balance, but vulnerable to becoming anxious or depressed if they're out of balance and overstressed by work or life.

Pitta, a mix of fire and water, tend to be passionate, intense natural-born leaders when they're in balance, but run the risk of becoming angry and judgmental when they are so single-mindedly involved in a project that they fail to take into account other people's views.

Kapha, a mix of earth and water, tend to be loving, accepting, and deeply thoughtful when they're in balance, but may be prone to melancholy or laziness when they're forced out of their usual routines.

To find out your own Ayurvedic type, or to check out some other non-western perspectives on personality, try some fun personality quizzes at gURL.com:
www.gurl.com/quizzes

According to Tali and Ophira Edut, astrologers, the personality traits associated with zodiac signs make people particularly well-suited for certain career paths:

SIGN	SOME CHARACTERISTIC TRAITS	SUITED TO CAREERS AS...
ARIES (March 21-April 19)	independent, self-sufficient	comedic actors, entrepreneurs, defense attorneys, holistic healers, professors, negotiators, salespeople, and military officers
TAURUSES (April 20 – May 20)	hardworking, determined	salon owners, engineers, film directors, bankers, singers, art dealers, and interior designers
GEMINIS (May 21 – June 20)	energetic, enthusiastic	editors, researchers, psychiatrists, brain surgeons, stand-up comedians, public relations agents, and detectives
CANCERS (June 21 – July 22)	nurturing, perceptive, self-protective	writers, editors, clothing designers, marine biologists, financial managers, restaurant owners, real estate brokers, professors, and nurses
LEOS (July 23 – August 22)	ego-driven, dramatic	movie stars, world leaders, filmmakers, coaches, bodyguards, language specialists, and playwrights
VIRGOS (August 23 – September 22)	generous, well-organized	therapists, nutritionists, accountants, critics, office managers, journalists, doctors, and architects
LIBRAS (September 23 – October 22)	charming, balanced	judges, party promoters, diplomats, food critics, fashion designers, massage therapists, novelists, and interior designers
SCORPIOS (October 23 – November 21)	feisty, passionate	dramatic actors, nightclub owners, real estate brokers, record producers, computer programmers, tax attorneys, surgeons, and spies
SAGITTARIANS (November 22 – December 21)	adventurous, truth-seeking	magazine publishers, pop stars, animal trainers, sales people, sportscasters, international newscasters, and motivational speakers
CAPRICORNS (December 22 – January 19)	loyal, hardworking	managers, politicians, police officers, doctors, presidents, school principals, and business owners
AQUARIANS (January 20 – February 18)	quick-thinking, stimulation-seeking	inventors, futurists, nonprofit workers, computer technicians, teachers, coaches, psychic healers, talk-show hosts, authors, and researchers
PISCES (February 19 – March 20)	sensitive, intuitive	therapists, nurses, graphic designers, photographers, filmmakers, actors, and massage therapists

THE OLD-FASHIONED GUT CHECK

Another low-tech but highly effective way to find out more about who you are and what you might want to do with your life is to start noticing which activities genuinely get you excited and involved. Scientists have spent a lot of time in recent years studying happiness, and one thing they've discovered is that life is meaningful and rewarding when we find ourselves regularly involved with tasks that are challenging (and sometimes intimidating at first), but ultimately totally absorbing. When we're fully engaged in certain activities—in a state of "flow," as scientists call it—we become committed to problem solving and learning everything we can about that particular task or pastime. And we end up naturally reinforcing and building upon our inherent skills. The intense pleasure of such all-consuming "flow" activities stems from the fact that they give people a regular, built-in reward—the satisfaction that comes with mastering new challenges.

So take a good, long look at your own life. Can you think of situations where you're totally swept up by what you're doing? What makes your heart race? Are there times when you find yourself so single-mindedly absorbed in something that you're surprised to look up at the clock and see that two hours just flew by? These experiences happen for different people at different times. But somewhere in your life, you're probably already involved with activities that can tell you a great deal about yourself—how you like to work, how you like to interact with people, and where your true talents lie. And it's very possible that these experiences will end up leading you toward the kind of work you'll want to be involved with throughout your life.

Interest Inventories

Many schools across the country offer standardized tests known as "interest inventories" to students as early as eighth or ninth grade. Generally, interest inventories are designed to help students take stock of their interests, then use the information they've gained to learn more about careers they might be well suited for and to find out about any academic requirements (in high school and beyond) needed to get there.

As with all tests, interest inventories have varying margins of error—which means you shouldn't regard their results as 100 percent accurate indicators of who you are or who you're destined to become. If your test results suggest that you'd enjoy a career in medicine but you can't stand the sight of blood, you obviously shouldn't feel obligated to follow that advice. Also, there are many career options that aren't even represented in the interest inventories. But it's still a good idea to take them if you can, since they can help you gain a clearer understanding of your preferences and capabilities and grasp the connections between your school assignments and the working world.

Check with your guidance counselor to see when interest inventories (such as the widely used ones described below) are being offered at your school or in your area. And, by all means, discuss your results with your guidance counselor, teachers, and parents afterward. It's possible that you may be on track for some of the careers you're beginning to consider. But it's also possible that you'll want to buckle down in certain courses now, or start looking into

As a kid, I was fascinated by everything, from the stars to pus. I wanted to know how things worked. I ended up studying engineering and Afro-American studies in college.

I try to fit in all of the things [in my work] that I am interested in. I have been a doctor in West Africa with the Peace Corps, an astronaut, and right now I have a number of projects. I have a technology consulting firm which helps engineering companies understand how they can work in developing countries. I am a professor of environmental studies at Dartmouth College, where I teach classes in technology and sustainable development. I also run an institute that's for advancing new technologies in developing countries. And I put together The Earth We Share, an international science camp for teenagers from all over the world . . . Much of what I do is coordinating with lots of people and doing research.

I think responsibility undergirds all my work—our responsibility to ourselves and our world.

DR. MAE JEMISON,
ENVIRONMENTAL ENGINEER, AND
FORMER NASA ASTRONAUT

I wanted to learn things that no one else knew, uncover secrets through patient observation. I wanted to come as close to talking to animals as I could.

JANE GOODALL, SCIENTIST

specific colleges or alternative post-secondary degrees that can help you accomplish your long-term goals, and you'll want to make sure everyone understands how your plans are unfolding in order to enlist their support as you move forward.

THE STRONG INTEREST INVENTORY

One of the best known interest tests is the Strong Interest Inventory. Originally developed in the twenties, the Strong has undergone many revisions over the years to reflect new research in career development. The current version is largely based on psychologist John Holland's theory that people with similar personalities like to be together and will enjoy similar occupations. As a young classification interviewer in the army, Dr. Holland noticed that people had remarkably similar traits and tastes. He later expanded this insight into his now-famous theory that people, their interests, and the type of work they prefer can be divided into six basic categories:

realistic (practical, hands-on, action-oriented)

investigative (academic, idea-oriented)

artistic (creative, flexible)

social (group-minded, helping)

enterprising
(competitive, business-oriented)

conventional
(organized, detail-oriented)

People taking the version of the Strong Profile for high school students are first asked to describe their relative like or dislike of various jobs, activities, and school subjects. Then they're asked to describe their own personal styles of leadership, working, learning, and risk-taking. When the results of the Strong come back, students can see which of

A quick, easy way to find out what kind of education or certification is required for the kind of work you're interested in is to look in the Occupational Outlook Handbook, the US Department of Labor's incredibly useful, information-packed career guide. Revised every two years, the OOH—available at most public libraries or online at www.bls.gov/oco/home.htm—also describes what workers in a wide range of occupations do on the job, what their working conditions are like, what they earn, and what the job prospects are in each specific field.

Holland's categories they appear to fit into best, and which types of work environments and types of jobs they might enjoy. Because the results are linked to jobs that require varying levels of education, the Strong can be helpful to both college-bound students and those who plan to start working right after high school.

REALISTIC
Mechanical Activities
Athletics
Military Activities
Agriculture
Nature

INVESTIGATIVE
Science
Mathematics
Medical Science

CONVENTIONAL
Data Management
Office Services
Computer Activities

HOLLAND'S HEXAGON

ARTISTIC
Culinary Arts
Writing
Music/Dramatics
Art
Applied Art

ENTERPRISING
Law/Politics
Public Speaking
Merchandising
Sales
Organizational Management

SOCIAL
Teaching
Medical Service
Religious Activities
Social Service

THE CAMPBELL INTEREST AND SKILL SURVEY

Whereas the Strong test is purely an interest inventory, the Campbell Interest and Skill Survey measures students' confidence in their own skills, in addition to their interest in specific occupations. The principle behind the test, created by psychologist David Campbell, is that people tend to do well in areas they find interesting and in which they feel confident in their abilities. Like the Strong, the Campbell test uses students' answers to generate reports pointing them toward clusters of jobs that generally correspond to Holland's six themes. But because the Campbell focuses on careers requiring post-secondary education, it is most helpful to students who are college bound.

THE PLAN TEST

Another interest inventory designed to help students start planning their futures is the aptly named PLAN test, which is mandatory in several states and typically taken by tenth graders. Created by ACT, the company that also puts out the ACT Assessment college admission test, PLAN measures students' aptitudes (their actual skills, as opposed to how they perceive their skills) alongside their interests. The PLAN test consists of multiple-choice questions in five different sections: English, Mathematics, Reading, Science, and a final section that asks you to name a specific career area that you think you might be interested in.

When your PLAN test results come back, they give you a good feel for how you're doing in school and suggest a group of related occupations—based on the combination of the career area you selected and your academic strengths and weaknesses—that you might want to explore. Since the aptitude portion of the PLAN test is similar to the ACT, many high school counselors encourage (or, again, require) their students to take it, because it has the added benefit of providing a chance to practice for the college admission test.

FOR A LIST OF BOOKS AND WEB SITES THAT LET YOU TAKE ERSONALITY TESTS SEE P. 17

Surveying the World

It is perfectly normal to have absolutely no clue about what you would like do after high school. Looking at overall trends in the US economy and industry can give you an idea what kinds of jobs might be easier to get. Of course, economic trends will come and go—so obviously the idea is to find something you're interested in or better yet, passionate about. It might be that your passions do intersect with areas of the economy that are desperate for new workers. If you are interested in any fields where there is a high demand, odds are that training in these areas may be easier and cheaper to come by—especially for women.

WOMEN AND TECHNOLOGY

We live in a world where technology is becoming more and more important and yet the number of women going into the technology fields is decreasing:

- Women constitute 46% of the workforce but only 23% of scientists and engineers.

- Of the ten fastest growing occupations, eight are math, science, or technology-related.

- In the next century, 65% of the economy will be based on information technology.

My mother filled our house with animal refugees. She used to say it doesn't matter who is suffering, it only matters that you can do something to help . . . .

In the early '70s, I happened into an animal shelter in Maryland, which was an extremely tough and dirty and inhumane place. It shocked me so much to see dogs and cats suffering in our so-called civilized part of the world that I left my job at the stock brokerage and entered the world of animal protection by applying for a job in this shelter, and trying to clean it up. In 1980, I was running the District of Columbia animal shelter and met Alexander Pechko, who had just returned from hunting down illegal whaling vessels in the Atlantic. And we put our knowledge of animal issues together and started PETA, which unexpectedly grew by leaps and bounds.

INGRID NEWKIRK,
HEAD OF PEOPLE FOR THE ETHICAL
TREATMENT OF ANIMALS (PETA)

I think success comes from being able to do what you love. Whether that's a career or raising children—or both—it's about being able to engage in something profound and meaningful every day.

THELMA GOLDEN,
ART CURATOR

I wasn't the typical future archaeologist who was always digging around in sandboxes. I wasn't all that enamored of dinosaurs, either. But I liked to hike and camp, and I guess I was a little bit prone to getting bored by things. So I really liked situations where you never knew what was going to happen or what you were going to discover, and archaeology is like that.

PATRICIA MCANANY,
PROFESSOR AND ARCHAEOLOGIST

When I was a kid, my brother and I would make believe that we were shooting films. We'd set up Jiffy peanut butter jars as lights—they used to be shiny and looked like movie lights. But we never filmed them.

When I was in high school, the only director I knew about was Hitchcock. When I learned that he had actually planned all those shots, I started watching his movies with a very different eye. I started imagining the "behind-the-scenes" of movies that I'd go see.

NANCY SAVOCA,
FILMMAKER

RESOURCES

Books

The Big Book of Personality Tests by Salvatore V. Didato, PhD (Black Dog & Leventhal) is a collection of one hundred illuminating and entertaining personality tests.

Discover What You're Best At by Linda Gale (Fireside) is a collection of aptitude tests that match your interests and skills to possible careers in a huge job directory.

Discovering Your Personality Type: The Essential Introduction to the Enneagram by Don Richard Riso and Russ Hudson (Mariner Books) contains the most recent version of the Riso-Hudson Enneagram Type Indicator (RHETI, version 2.5), plus practical information on how each personality type navigates everyday situations.

Do What You Are: Discover the Perfect Career for You through the Secrets of Personality Type by Paul D. Tieger and Barbara Barron-Tieger (Little, Brown & Company). A bible for students and adults looking for meaningful work, it explores the sixteen personality types defined by the famous Myers-Briggs Type Indicator (MBTI) and occupations that might be gratifying for each type.

Essential Ayurveda: What It Is and What It Can Do for You by Shubhra Krishan (New World Library) is a thorough, thought-provoking introduction to Ayurvedic health and life philosophy.

Flow: The Psychology of Optimal Experience by Mihaly Csikszentmihalyi (Perennial) is a best-selling exploration of different ways people find deep satisfaction in everyday life.

Web Sites

Discover Your Personality at http://www.discoveryourpersonality.com offers both the Strong Interest Inventory and the Myers-Briggs Type Indicator online for a fee.

The Enneagram Institute at http://www.enneagraminstitute.com offers a free sample of the Riso-Hudson Enneagram Type Indicator, and a longer version for a fee.

Humanmetrics.com at http://www.humanmetrics.com offers a free, fun, (and admittedly, not entirely reliable) online personality test based on Jung's type theory.

Jonathan Cainer, an astrologer who doesn't take himself too seriously, provides thought-provoking daily horoscopes and longer in-depth profiles of each zodiac sign at http://www.cainer.com.

considering your circumstances

For better or for worse, what YOU want to do with your life is only part of the story. In an ideal world, all of us would be able to pursue our dreams single-mindedly, without worrying about logistics or how it might affect the people around us. In the real world, all of us are subject to factors in our lives, and these impact the decisions we make. The circumstances of your life can dramatically affect the options that are available to you, shaping the decisions you make and the directions you take.

It's rare that a person feels totally free to choose any path without being affected by beliefs (whether individual or family-driven), responsibilities, money, or physical or cultural restrictions. Even if everyone around you is managing to keep their mouths shut about what you want to do with your life, it's likely that some idea of what "they" want you to do, or what you "should" do, is lurking somewhere in your mind. Your task is to figure out which of these things really matter to you, and how to reconcile your life circumstances with your life goals.

Figuring out to what degree your circumstances can/should/must affect your life path is one of the most difficult aspects of growing up. The first step is doing an inventory of what's going on in your life. Taking a good, honest look at what kind of situation you are in will give you the best perspective and help you find a balance between what your life demands and what you want to do with it.

What Are Your Circumstances?

EXPECTATIONS

People expect things of you. These expectations can be as general as making good decisions or taking the feelings of others into account, or as specific as choosing the college or career that a parent has determined is the right one for you, regardless of your own goals. When others have expectations about how you will live your life, it is often hard to separate those ideas from your own hopes for your future. How much you are affected by others' expectations depends on many factors—your relationship with the people expressing the expectations, how these expectations are expressed, how strong your own convictions are, and how close others' expectations are to the things you imagine for yourself. You might feel like if you ignore the things others have in mind for you, you're letting them down, which can be especially painful when they're people you care about. When your goals and others' expectations are in conflict, you have to find a way to resolve that dissonance. But, remember that you and only you own your future.

The following questions can help you to focus on whose expectations are guiding your decisions:

ask yourself

>> **What are your expectations for yourself? Why?**

>> What do you think your parents' expectations of you are? (Ask them if you're not sure.) Is meeting their expectations important to you? Why or why not?

>> **What are your teachers' expectations of you?**

>> What do your friends expect you to do with your future? Do they try to influence you in any way? How?

>> **Think about how all of these people might be influencing you and why. There is no formula that tells you what to do, but it is helpful to be aware of all of the factors that shape your decisions.**

I worked to help with the bills because my dad died.

Everyone feels a different degree of responsibility to those around them. Some people, for example, feel that they must meet the expectations of the people they care about, because they feel that the risk of disappointing them is too great. Others feel freer to follow their own paths, either because the people around them don't express strong expectations, or because they have less fear of rejecting them.

But what is real responsibility, and to whom are you really responsible? Some of the stuff we think of as responsibility is actually more like guilt. The reality is that your parents may want certain things for you, but unless you've made an explicit deal—in which, for example, they agree to support you if you pursue a certain path—your feelings of responsibility are based on emotions, not obligation. Emotional responsibility is a powerful force which has impacted many a person's choices throughout life. It is never smart to ignore the feelings of people who matter in your life. But it is also important to differentiate real responsibility from the desire not to hurt people's feelings by making the choice you think is right for you (rather than the one they expect you to make). Figuring out which is which can get complicated.

>> **Who am I hurting if I make this choice?**

>> Am I just disappointing someone, or will there be a substantial loss?

>> **Are the people in question dependent on me for any reason?**

>> Will making my choice impact their lives in ways they won't be able to handle?

>> **Am I able to handle their feelings in whatever way they may be expressed?**

>> Will I feel resentful if I choose to accept their plans for me instead of pursuing my own?

>> **Is there a compromise I can live with?**

Some situations may be more clear-cut than others. If you care for a less able person, contribute to the household finances, have a role in the family business, or have a family of your own (see below for more on these specific situations), your decisions impact others in a way that goes beyond expectations and emotions. But in many family situations, the distinction between real responsibility, emotional expectations, and guilt is more subtle. It's up to you to explore the feelings and realities associated with your goals and determine which decision makes the most sense for you.

> I decided to go to community college because I was offered a good babysitting job for the school year and I didn't mind living at home and going to school close by.
> (Anne Arundel Community College, Arnold, MD)

RELATIONSHIPS

Expectations and feelings of responsibility aren't limited to family ties. Close friends will be affected by your choices as well, and they might have ideas about what decisions you should make. People who are close often want to stay that way, and your friends might be pressuring you to go to a school that keeps you close together, or discouraging you from moving far away to pursue your plans. It can be difficult not to feel guilty about what you want to do if it separates you from people who were once the core of your emotional life. On the other hand, choosing a path that doesn't fulfill your needs and goals just so you can stay close to your friends won't be gratifying either.

> My best friend had to go there, so I went. Big mistake. The first year there we fought and weren't friends. Don't choose a school based on a friend and/or boyfriend/girlfriend. Just because they are going doesn't mean you have to go there. I spent the first year of college alone, not knowing anyone.
> (Northeast Technical Community College, Norfolk, NE)

Both my parents paid a lot of attention to the news. I also loved reading books, and I figured out that I wanted to be a writer pretty early. But I knew that for the few novelists that are very wealthy, there are a lot that are struggling, and I wanted more of a day-to-day existence, to make a living as a writer. So I thought about being a journalist.

TAMALA EDWARDS, JOURNALIST

HOW I GOT HERE

The transition from high school to the years beyond can be very taxing on friendships and other relationships. People do grow apart, and it is true that the choices people make have a direct impact on how hard it is to maintain closeness. When people are immersed in different worlds, it's natural to drift apart. But friendships are fluid, and when they do fluctuate, it's not always a direct cause-and-effect situation.

Romantic relationships can also impact your decisions. Sometimes people don't want to go to a school that's too far away from a significant other. Other times, people want to make a fresh start, to reinvent themselves in a place where they don't know anybody and nobody knows them.

What keeps people together is not just geography and similar experiences, but a real desire and effort on both people's parts to bridge the gaps that may be caused by being in different places, both physically and emotionally. Moving from the known world of high school to the unknown afterwards affects different people in different ways. Many close high school friends have gone on to college together expecting to stay best friends, only to find that each found herself adjusting to her new environment in a different way, and that their friendship wasn't intended to go on unchanged. It's important to remember that your evolution and your life path is your own, and while your friends are important to you now, and may be important to you for the rest of your life, you need to choose your path according to your own goals, not theirs.

I wanted and needed to stay close to my family, especially my mother.

I wanted to be close to my boyfriend, who is stationed at Fort Bragg, North Carolina.
(University of North Carolina, Chapel Hill)

FINANCIAL ISSUES

Higher education, training programs, and travel all come at some cost. But the amazing thing about leaving high school to move onto whatever's next is that there are many resources out there and places to turn for financial support. If your family doesn't have the financial resources to help you much as you move into the next phase of your life, you have to be that much more creative and more resourceful.

When it comes to thinking about your financial needs (both immediate and long-term), it is important not to make short-term decisions that will hinder you in achieving all your dreams. Any education, training, or travel experience is part of the long-term investment you are making in yourself and your potential earnings. If you have family members you need to support, it can be even more difficult to sort out your long-term planning versus immediate financial needs. It is important not to start from the point of view that things are off-limits to you if you have substantial short-term financial needs. Where there is a need, there is a way. You may have to take a longer or less desirable path to get to where you want to go, but it is worth it to investigate all options and leads before deciding something is unattainable.

I chose my college because it was a lot cheaper than Baylor and they also have a good med program. I'm still glad that I went to Lamar.
(Lamar University, Beaumont, TX)

ALSO SEE CHAPTER 8, FINANCING YOUR DREAM, ON PP. 166–177.

It was in my price range and the best I could get for my money—it's the best school in my state, and the 30th top state school in the country. It's often called the "Ivy League" of state schools.
(State University of New York, Binghamton)

I wanted to go to school in Pittsburgh, and of the two schools I applied to, both accepted me but only Duquesne offered me a scholarship. It was an incredibly generous academic scholarship, and even though I didn't like the atmosphere of the school so much, I had to sacrifice a little bit of satisfaction in order to pay for a college education.
(Duquesne University, Pittsburgh, PA)

HOW I GOT HERE

I still remember the first time I asked my mother if I could go to college. She said, hesitating, "If you can get a scholarship, you can go." Her mouth said, "If you can get a scholarship," but her eyes said that she didn't think it would happen.

RUTH SIMMONS, PRESIDENT, BROWN UNIVERSITY

RELIGIOUS BELIEFS

An important thing to consider in determining the path you take is whether or not you have strong or specific spiritual beliefs. If your belief system or religious practice is shared by your family, you may have given little thought to the logistics of maintaining it. There are many issues to consider, including whether or not you feel it is important to be around others who share your beliefs. There are numerous educational institutions that are strongly identified with different religious and/or ethnic groups. Most colleges and universities have a range of religiously-affiliated clubs and living situations. If your beliefs require you to observe specific dietary or behavioral rules, you will need to keep these in mind when choosing where you want to live and what kind of environment is right for you. You may also choose to maintain your religious and spiritual life independently, outside of a formally supportive setting. If you make this choice and your family is very invested in your religious identity, be aware that it may take some work to make them comfortable with your decision. In the end, your spiritual life is your own, and it is important that you consider your own wishes first and foremost as you continue on your adult path.

> The church that I go to, Maryland Christian Fellowship, is located on campus, so when I was living in the dorms, I could easily get up on Sundays to go. I've been able to hang in there because of it.
> (University of Maryland, College Park)

FOR INFORMATION ON RELIGIOUSLY-AFFILIATED SCHOOLS, SEE P. 65

PREGNANCY AND MOTHERHOOD

Having a child while pursuing other goals in your life presents particular challenges. Pregnancy can make it physically and emotionally difficult to concentrate on study or work; caring for a child is a huge responsibility and a full-time job in itself. If you are the primary care giver for a child or children, you may find that you have little time to pursue other interests, especially those that don't contribute to the financial bottom line of your household. Childcare frees up parents to work and study, but many moms find it hard to afford the cost unless they have high-paying jobs. You may need to seek out jobs that offer flexible schedules and nontraditional education options. Some schools or programs offer subsidized

> I looked after my child, who I had when I was only thirteen. It's rewarding to see something you created grow. I work at KFC full-time. And some nights I work late shifts at the call center downtown. It pretty much sucks, but I am looking into furthering my education possibly by night school.

childcare. Working or studying at home is a good compromise for many parents. Childcare co-ops are also an option—check around your school or neighborhood to look for other young parents with similar needs. Although the circumstances may make it more difficult, having a child does not have to stand in the way of your education or career. Negotiating a balance between family and other aspects of your life is an ongoing process.

I got married and had a baby. I am very much in love with the guy I married and I love my two sons very much . . . but I feel very tied down sometimes. I plan to start college as soon as my husband gets back from an overseas military tour.

PHYSICAL DISABILITIES AND ILLNESS

If you have a physical disability, a learning disability, or an illness, you may need to think more carefully about your post–high school choices. The good thing is that there are numerous resources and places to turn for help. The hard part is that it is usually up to you to seek out the assistance you will need. It's important to have a very intimate understanding of exactly what your needs are, so you can be totally articulate and best represent the things you need in order to make the most of any learning environment. You are your own best advocate.

The first half of the year, I took the time off to undergo major surgery and I needed time to recover. I started college the second half of the year.

If you have a physical disability, it is essential to research the best schools or programs for people with your condition. The Americans with Disabilities Act (ADA) was established to ensure that public places are accessible, but only you can best understand if and how a certain environment will allow you to do the things you want to do. There is a tremendous range of compliance among schools and programs, so definitely make an on-site visit. It can be helpful to seek out other people with similar disabilities, who may have strategic ideas to share.

If you have an illness, it will be important to make this clear to anyone you are working with as you pursue your future plans, so you can set up a situation that makes sense given your specific medical needs.

I actually was supposed to graduate in '02, but due to some medical problems, ended up getting my GED in April of '03. But I'll tell you, that doesn't make a damn difference. I'm going to college in Boston this fall, and I'm living proof that you can do anything you put your mind to.

LEARNING DISABILITIES

If you've been dealing with learning disabilities in high school, you already know how important it is to find the best available resources. Although the Individuals with Disabilities Education Act (IDEA) provides funding for schools, and schools are required to accommodate people with learning disabilities, finding a good situation is up to you. The types of services available can vary widely from school to school. Some schools, such as Curry College in Massachusetts and the University of Hartford in Connecticut, are known for having strong programs for students with learning disabilities.

To find the best learning environment for you, first turn to the resources at your high school (your guidance counselor, tutor, teacher, or department head) to understand which options can be tailored to your particular learning issues. It's also important to be re-evaluated during your senior year so that you'll have all the appropriate, and most up-to-date, paperwork at hand when you take the next step.

SPECIAL NEEDS RESOURCES

- Landmark College in Vermont is the only school that was established specifically for students with learning disabilities.
- *Colleges With Programs for Students with Learning Disabilities or Attention Deficit Disorders* (Peterson's Guides) is an excellent reference to specific programs at more than 750 two- and four-year colleges.

FAMILY BUSINESS

Everyone's family has some kind of expectations about her future, but this concern is magnified when there is a business to consider.

If you are already a working part of the business, that may have a direct impact on your decision about whether or where to go to school, and under what circumstances (e.g., part-time, full-time, night or day classes). If you plan to join the business at some point in the future, that may inform your choice of a major or a specific area of study. If your family expects you to join a business that has been in the family for generations (or one that a parent has built from scratch), but you'd rather do something else, there may be serious issues to reconcile. If you're already part of the business and want to move on, you'll need to determine with your family what the impact of your departure would be. If you truly cannot be replaced,

I have no long-term plans at all; I'm just enjoying my youth. I tell my family that I want to be a biologist, but that's just to get them off my back. I think eventually I might want to take over the restaurant and manage it myself.

perhaps you can find a way to continue your role in the business while working toward your other career goals. Rejecting the family business in search of a different future can have a serious emotional impact as well as a logistical and financial one. Your family may feel that you are rejecting them and criticizing their way of life by choosing something different for yourself. Being sensitive to these feelings will help you work toward a solution that will keep both your family's business and your own dreams afloat. Even if you think that your final destiny will be to join the family business, you may be able to convince your family that taking some time for yourself to do something totally unrelated will increase the value you bring to the family venture.

CHAPTER 3.

gathering information

One of the most empowering and useful life skills is the ability to research—to track down information and people who can help you understand how the world works. As you contemplate your future, you might feel nervous about all the unknown variables that lie ahead of you. But even if it all feels overwhelming right now, it is definitely possible to start to get answers to some of the confusing yet important questions you face. Research can help you figure out where and what you want to study, or where you want to live and work.

How to Research

To be a great researcher, you will need to gather points of view from a lot of different people; read a variety of books and articles (on paper and the Internet); and, perhaps most importantly, you'll need to be persistent. It's important to keep on asking questions until you're sure that you've heard enough different opinions and verified all the facts, so you can make your own decisions with confidence. Your persistence will pay off. With strong life-sleuthing skills, you will be able to determine what steps you'll need to take to get yourself into a certain school, or to increase the chance of getting the job you want, or to do whatever it is you want to do.

Occasionally, you'll hear adults lament the opportunities they missed in life. "I just did what I was told. I never knew you could do anything else." But the fact is, people can accomplish amazing things in their lives if they keep their eyes and ears open and do some determined digging.

Cultivate curiosity. Become the kind of person who soaks up information, from multiple sources, like a sponge. Ask questions, get answers. It's a remarkably simple strategy, but it will help you understand the broadest range of options available to you and help you define and move ever closer to your own goals. An added benefit of being naturally curious is that it will put you into contact with interesting new people and ideas throughout your entire lifetime. You may also be surprised to discover how much information you can gather by just staying open rather than tuning people out. Don't rule out research by osmosis.

EXPLORE YOUR OPTIONS ONLINE

With a wealth of information readily available online, researching is easier than ever before. Every school, many companies and trade groups, and almost every city has its own Web site full of detailed information and helpful links to related sites. Chances are, you've already used the Internet to research school projects and topics relating to your hobbies or other interests. The process of learning more about specific schools, jobs, or places you might like to live will be much the same. Some of the trails you'll follow online will ultimately be dead ends, but others will dramatically expand your knowledge of the subject you're exploring. One note of caution about collecting information online: after consulting commercial Web sites (those that are trying to sell a specific product or service), be sure to compare their information with information you gather from outside sources. For example, if you're researching a specific college, find

> I researched on the Internet because you can research everything about schools all at your own pace.
> (University of New Hampshire, Durham)

out what the generic college guidebooks have to say about the school as well as whatever the school may have to say about itself. You may also find valuable "inside" information on students' personal websites or blogs.

USE YOUR LOCAL LIBRARY

In addition to their newer role of providing computers and free Internet access, libraries are a fantastic source of well-organized, well-chosen books on thousands of topics, including some that are probably on your mind right now: careers, schools, travel, or starting your own business. You may find that your high school library has a lot of books that can help you research your options for the future, but be sure to expand your horizons to check out public libraries in your area, too.

My mom bought every book ever written on college hunting. She was the best help.

To get the lay of the land at your local library, ask a librarian to give you a tour of the stacks where the books you're looking for are located, and to teach you how to use the library's catalogue system, so you can look up books by title, author, or subject on your own, and request books from other branches in your library's system, if need be. And by all means, be sure to ask the librarian if there are any books on the subject you're researching that he or she can particularly recommend. Librarians field questions and get feedback from readers every day, so they tend to know which books are popular and which ones aren't worth the paper they're printed on.

SEEK EXPERT ADVICE

If you come across some information that doesn't make sense to you, it might be a good time to find an expert to talk to. There are plenty of people out there who are professionally obligated—or who volunteer their time—to help people like you find their way in the world, and all you need to do is reach out to them for information and advice. Your high school probably has a guidance counselor who knows a good deal about

HOW I GOT HERE

I grew up in LA and wanted to be an actress. I thought that's what girls did in movies. I finally started taking photos, then making short films, when I was seventeen after an inspirational trip to Rome. I went [to Rome] to be an actress. My personality type liked looking instead of being looked at.

I love preparation. Research is one of my favorite things about making a film. Researching the characters, the location design, the look for a film, everything about it.

TAMRA DAVIS, FILM DIRECTOR

schools, jobs, and other options available to people your age, and she should be the first expert you consult. If you haven't already, make an appointment to speak with her ASAP.

In addition to helping you assess your options based on your interests, grades, and financial situation, your school counselor should be able to tell you about upcoming education and career fairs to be held at your high school or in your area. It's a good idea to attend these, as they will introduce you to people who work in the fields or at the schools you'd like to explore. It's also a good idea to go to all counseling sessions and fairs with paper and a pen to jot down names and phone numbers. And don't be shy about making follow-up calls whenever you need more information (something easier said than done—but definitely worth it). People interested in promoting their profession will be glad to explain things to you, and school admissions officers are paid to field calls.

Finally, if you've already spoken to your school's counselor and want to learn more—or you'd just like to hear what someone else has to say—you can also consult (for a price) with an independent career or college counselor. (Ask around or look in your local yellow pages under "career and vocational counseling" or "college counseling" for the names of people who do this kind of work in your area.) In some places, libraries and community centers also offer free seminars for young people interested in exploring post-high school education and careers. Check with your local librarian to see if such a service is offered in your area, and by all means, take advantage of it if you can—it's another great way of meeting experts who can help shed light on some of the options you may be considering.

One of my teachers actually acted like my counselor. Coming from a small community, she knew me very well both inside and outside of school, so she was able to help me pick the best school for me.

(Colorado College, Colorado Springs)

A high school counselor for kids of color trying to go on to college was the most helpful resource for me. My counselor helped me fill out my application, scheduled my interview, and even brought me to the interview herself! My mentor and her husband both graduated from my school; it was very close to home, and it was an art school with all of the programs I was looking for.

(Minneapolis College of Art and Design, MN)

My most helpful resource was my guidance counselor. He knew all about the process, and had helped many other students do it. I could ask all the questions that I wanted and didn't have to look it up in a book or on the Internet; I could just get a response from a person!

(Providence College, RI)

MAKING CONNECTIONS

The most effective way to gain an understanding of a particular situation is to consult someone who's been there. If you don't happen to already know someone personally who has firsthand experience with a job or school you're curious about, you'll need to reach out to someone you don't know.

Coming in to college the best people to get advice from were the upper classmen. They'll tell you if a professor speaks in a monotone or where the best jobs are.
(Concordia University, Seward, NE)

Different people have different levels of comfort when it comes to contacting strangers, or even acquaintances, and asking them for help or advice. Some people feel comfortable asking people to help them get into a school or land a certain internship or job, while others feel timid about taking up too much of someone's time. But it's very important to be bold at this point in your life (or anytime you're facing a transition in the future) and try to make connections with people who have graduated from schools you're interested in or who work in fields that you'd like to explore. If you're more naturally shy, it can be helpful to remember that most people really do love to talk about themselves.

Friends of friends who've graduated from the schools you're considering and local alumni admissions representatives (people who've agreed to talk to prospective students for their school and whose contact information can be found through the schools' admissions offices), as well as current and past employees of companies or firms, are the best people to give you the inside scoop on what a certain college/job/internship is all about. With the information you gain through speaking with them, you'll be able to make the strongest case possible for yourself if you decide to apply. Furthermore, the people you form connections with can also personally recommend you to the employer/school—something that could potentially tip a decision in your favor.

Getting any foot in the door

It's a fact of life that people who have more connections have an easier time gaining entry into many situations—especially in the work world. To be sure, there's a lot of nepotism—favoritism shown to some people because of family or social connections—in the world. But the fact is, employers and college admissions officers do respect the input of people who have worked at or graduated from their institutions, so it is helpful to connect with people who have an affiliation with any institution or organization that you'd like to be a part of. And as long as your inquiry is respectful and serious, your effort to enlist somebody's help won't be construed as you simply asking them to pull strings for you. Here are some basic guidelines for contacting people who may be able to help you achieve your educational and professional goals:

1. **Whenever you call or write someone asking for a favor, introduce yourself right away and ask if you can take a minute of their time.** Explain who you are, how you got their name (or how and where you met if you've spoken before), and, in one sentence, the reason why you're contacting them now.

FOR MORE INFORMATION ON PROFESSIONAL NETWORKING, SEE P. 139–141.

2. **Whether your request is for an informational interview or a letter of recommendation (or some other favor), make clear early in your call or letter that you understand the person you're contacting has "many other obligations" and that they may not be able to help you.** That way, you're giving them a way to bow out gracefully if they're too busy or have a conflict of interest—such as having already agreed to write a letter of recommendation for somebody else.

3. **In clear, concise language, elaborate on the reason why you're contacting this person.** If it's for an informational interview, explain what you specifically want to find out about a school or job. If it's for a recommendation letter, explain why you think you're well suited to the school or job in question. (The point of this step is to give the person you're trying to connect with a way to connect to you—a place to begin the conversation when you later speak face-to-face, or some talking points for a recommendation letter they may write in your behalf.)

4. **Follow up with a thank-you note or phone call.** Since many people don't bother to say thank you—leaving those who help them feeling a bit miffed about the energy they spent in their behalf—you can easily distinguish yourself with simple words of gratitude to the people who help you as you move forward in life. Arguably, the appreciation people get for helping others is part of what makes them willing to keep on doing it. So you can think of it as a moral obligation to do your part to make sure the system you've benefited from remains in place.

Decision

There are innumerable theories about the best way to make decisions in life. In China, people toss coins onto a chart filled with symbols—known as the I Ching—for advice on how to go forth into the future. In India, people who follow the Hindu faith believe in reincarnation and the concept of karma, which holds that a person's fate in one lifetime has already been determined by what happened in a previous lifetime. In many parts of the world (including here in the US), some people seek advice from horoscopes and psychics to help them plot love and career moves.

You may have a system of your own—based on the stars, the stock market, opinions of people you trust, your grandma's favorite adage, or any other kind of information that's important to you—for making decisions. But it is a good idea to spend some time, now and whenever you're at a crossroads in life, thinking about the degree of control you have over your future and how you personally can bring about the changes you'd like to bring about for yourself.

Most of the time, things happen in life through some combination of fate and free will. There are things that you can't control—such as a chance meeting that leads to a successful job interview (for better) or a bad case of the flu that makes you seem kind of dumb your first day on the job (for worse). And there are things that you can control—you can decide to write a lackluster, half-hearted job-application letter that's quickly passed over, or you can choose to spend more time crafting an eye-catching letter that serves as an example of the kind of detail-oriented, master communicator you'd be in the job (perhaps landing yourself the job).

There is a great deal of mystery working in the world all the time, and there will be occurrences that you could have had no way of foreseeing—which means that you can't beat yourself up when your best-laid plans don't work out the way you hoped they would. (It happens to everybody.) But you can also make smart, responsible decisions in life that will probably work out quite nicely for you. Finding a comfortable balance between conscious decision making and peaceful acceptance can be tricky, but it's important to recognize the value of both sides of the coin.

Making

The following questions will help you to learn more about your personal style of decision making:

ask yourself

>> **Are you superstitious?**

>> Is there someone whose advice you trust above all others'? If so, what do you admire about the way this person makes decisions?

>> **What's one of the toughest decisions you've ever made? What were the circumstances that made that decision so difficult?**

>> Have you ever made a decision you regret? How would you choose to handle the situation differently, if you could?

>> **Are you impulsive, or do you take your time weighing various options before you finally decide what you want to do?**

>> Do you tend to fret over decisions after you've made them, worrying about whether or not you did the right thing?

>> **Are you more or less content with your choices, no matter how things turn out?**

>> Is there a decision you made recently that you're particularly proud of?

LIVING WITH THE CONSEQUENCES OF YOUR DECISIONS

Whether you are 100 percent sure of your choice or totally indecisive about what to do next, it is important to remember that this is just one choice of millions about your future. For example, if you are deciding whether or not to go to college, and you decide yes, then there will be decisions about which college, which classes, which dorm, which activities, with one choice leading naturally to more options.

Your choices can affect how you see yourself, and how others see you. For example, people who decide against going to college sometimes feel self-conscious around those who are more educated. And those who attend particularly prestigious schools may have to contend with others assuming they're snobbish. You have to determine for yourself whether your concern about the opinions of others is important enough to

Another tough thing about college is: You have no idea how much college makes you change your mind! In my first year/first semester, I originally was a Theatre major, with a minor in Sociology. Semester after that, I changed to a double major in Theatre and Journalism. Sophomore year during the summer, I decided to major in Journalism and minor in Theatre. Currently, I'm missing theatre a lot and almost want to be a double-major in Theatre and Journalism again ... I just want to make sure that I make the right choice!

(University of Kansas, Lawrence)

impact your decision—as well as whether you yourself will feel good about your choices.

It is also important to remember that very few decisions are irreversible. You always have the option of transferring schools (if you're not happy with the one you've selected), taking a year off (if you're not ready for school after all), switching jobs (if you've taken on an unpleasant one), and studying abroad or volunteering (if you need a change of pace).

You can and should do as much as possible to educate yourself so that the decisions you make are informed, thoughtful ones. You should know that if you decide not to go on with your schooling, certain jobs may be harder for you to get. You should know that if you decide to go to college, then you're probably going to have to work pretty hard to stay in. In other words, there are consequences to your decisions. But you will only know (for sure) where a particular path is going to lead after you follow it.

DEALING WITH DISAPPOINTMENT

Getting knocked off the path you expect to follow can throw you for a loop, but it can also be a great chance to explore new directions. Taking rejection in stride is never easy, but here are some things that can help you feel more positive about taking a different road than the one you planned for.

Grieve the loss, then move on. Once you've given yourself the time to be upset about not getting what you thought you wanted, give yourself the freedom to move on. Being rejected by your school or job of choice is always painful. But ask anyone who's been there whether they still regret it and you'll have a hard time finding people who wish they'd gotten the nod instead of the no.

Don't take it personally. Schools and jobs receive tens to hundreds to thousands of applications for every available spot. It's impossible to know what goes into each decision, but you can take heart in the knowledge that there's a far greater chance that your rejection was the result of a competitive environment than your personal lack. You will probably never know why you weren't chosen ... and it won't do you much good to spend time wondering. If you know you gave your best efforts to the application, it can be helpful to consider that what got someone in instead of you wasn't about being better, but about being different, and maybe more in line with what the people making the decision were looking for.

Forgive yourself. If you do happen to know that you screwed up somehow—didn't give the essay your all, really botched an interview, or otherwise directly compromised your application process—acknowledge the goof-up and let it go. In situations like these, there's probably some underlying reason you weren't 100 percent dedicated to the goal at hand. Maybe you felt pressured to apply and didn't really want to, or maybe you don't feel you deserved to be accepted. It's in your best interest to consider these and other possibilities that might have contributed to your poor performance, and then to move forward with a commitment to giving the future your best shot.

Keep an open mind. Even if you had your heart set on something that isn't going to happen, try to remember that the loss of this opportunity makes room for a whole new set of possibilities. It really is true that when one door closes another one opens. When you look back on this bump in the road, you'll be much more likely to feel grateful than resentful about the unexpected rerouting . . . and you won't be able to imagine your life any other way.

Try, try again. If you really had your heart set on a certain situation, don't forget that you can always try again at the next opportunity. Just because you don't make it on the first try doesn't mean you need to abandon all hope. Persistence can sometimes pay off, and repeated applications show commitment, which is always a plus.

PART 2.
THE NEXT STEP

Once you have made your decision—whether it's school of some sort, work, travel, or a combination of things—you will need to focus your energy on making it happen. It's time to close the chapter on the hard work of deciding what to do and get organized about how to do it.

This time in your life is most likely extremely busy and frenetic. Organization is truly your best friend when it comes to planning your future. There are going to be a number of specific things to consider depending on what decision you have made. Make sure that you are aware of all the requirements for any program, job, or opportunity as well as all the deadlines to ensure that you will be able to participate. This is not an easy thing to do, and for many people this might be the first time in their lives they will take on such a large responsibility.

Don't underestimate the amount of time it will take you to do all the preparation required by any opportunity—but try to not be overwhelmed by the tasks. In many cases it all seems harder than it really is when you sit down and get to work. The most important thing that you will need to communicate to any employers, admissions committee, or program is that you are a good candidate. The clearer you feel about why you are doing something, the better. But even if you don't know exactly why you want to be a zoology major or a bartender, communicating your enthusiasm for an opportunity can go a long way in getting you noticed.

While you are actively pursuing opportunities, stress may creep into your life in many ways. This process itself is stressful, but like anything, staying balanced will keep you from making rash moves and decisions that might hurt your chances of getting what you want. You may also be facing quite a bit of competition, depending

on what your goals are. Remaining focused about what you want to do and confident about your strong points can help steer you through this time.

The following chapters will give you more details about the various options available on any given path; practical advice on implementing your decision; and comments and advice from people who've made a similar choice.

four-year colleges

College is a unique opportunity to spend your time learning about whatever interests you, experiencing new things, and meeting new people. For these reasons and more, it is often a great choice and a privelege for those who are able to attend. A college degree also opens doors. In many careers, it is a requirement.

College is also a great place to make friendships and other connections that can benefit you socially and professionally for the rest of your life. College can be very expensive, but it's usually an investment that pays back immeasurably throughout your life. Annual earnings for those with a college degree are sixty percent higher than for those with only a high school diploma. Over the course of a lifetime, a college grad earns one million dollars more on average than someone without a bachelor's degree.

Choosing a College

The first step is to figure out which schools you might like to apply to. Applying to college is costly and time-consuming. You'll increase your chances of getting into the school you want to go to if you apply to fewer schools, and really focus your energy on those applications. Ask yourself the following questions to help narrow down the list of potential schools.

ask yourself

>> Where would you like to live? At home? Nearby, or far from home?

>> Do you see yourself in an urban or a rural setting?

>> Do you think you'd be most comfortable at a big school with lots of variety or in a smaller, more intimate setting?

>> What subjects interest you? Are there schools with a particularly strong reputation in your field of study?

>> Do you play sports? Do you have other interests that are an important part of your life?

>> Do you work and learn best in a structured environment, or do you prefer more freedom?

UNIVERSITY VS. COLLEGE

When deciding on schools, some people factor in whether a school has graduate programs (universities) or exists solely for those seeking a bachelor's degree (colleges). There are advantages and disadvantages to each. In a university, you may have the option to take graduate classes. You may also be able to apply for some sort of combination undergrad/graduate degree program where you earn a master's and bachelor's degree simultaneously in, say, five years—which is less time than it would take you to complete both degrees individually. Union College is famous for its eight-year med program, which combines pre-med and medical school classes in a condensed period of time. Students at the University of Pennsylvania can earn a BS and an MBA in only five years.

I started out being enrolled full-time, but I found it too stressful, so I cut back to only taking three classes a semester, which allowed me to concentrate and get things done more efficiently.
(Minneapolis College of Art and Design, MN)

If you really know what you want to do, and it involves an advanced degree, it might make sense to give yourself the option of either getting a jump on your coursework, or even trying out some graduate classes. Another advantage of universities is that they provide a broader student body. For some, the number of students can be overwhelming, and size becomes a distinct disadvantage to certain universities. Another downside is that you will likely wind up with teaching assistants (TAs) teaching your classes, or running smaller sections of big lecture classes. TAs can be very intelligent and engaging. But they probably haven't been at it for very long, and may also be preoccupied with their own coursework.

At colleges, the focus and services are geared toward undergraduates. For some people, this smaller universe and more accessible support system are distinct advantages.

POSTPONING SCHOOL

There are lots of people who wind up going to college but don't do so right out of high school. Some people don't get into their school of choice right away and opt to intern or volunteer or do some other interesting work that might improve their chances of getting in the following year. Others defer admission—apply and are accepted to a school, then take a year to work, travel, or deal with a personal issue before attending. Still others simply take some time to experience the real world before they decide that they would like some more formal education. For most schools, it doesn't matter if you apply right out of high school or later on, and you will get much more out of school when you are really ready to begin.

Four Years—More or Less

Going to a four-year college doesn't necessarily mean you'll have a bachelor's degree in four years. Some students are eager to get on with their lives, or with advanced degrees, so they load up on courses and/or go to summer school and finish in three or three and a half years. Some people take time off—to travel, launch a business, or just mellow out after a particularly stressful year. Others take a lighter course load to make time for work or to ease the pressure (though this route

- Bethel College in Kansas guarantees a bachelor's degree in four years; if you don't finish it by then, your additional courses are free!

- In private schools, 52 percent of students graduate in four years. For public schools, the figure is 24 percent.

- Among public institutions, West Point ranks highest in four-year-college rates at 86 percent. University of Virginia is next with 84 percent.

can be particularly expensive if you pay by the semester). While 37 percent of students enrolled in college do graduate in four years, it's good to be open to the possibility that this particular leg of your journey might take more or less time.

WHAT'S YOUR TYPE?

There are schools to suit every personality and academic orientation. Finding a school with the right vibe for you—and the kind of students you want to hang out with—is every bit as important as finding the school that offers the best classes for your field of study. For some people, it's even more important to get the right personality match. Lots of learning happens outside of the classroom.

What follows are just some of the types of schools you might want to consider. The categories we've come up with are qualitative, personality-driven characterizations designed to help you think about what might be the most comfortable and stimulating environment for you. This is not a comprehensive listing, by any means.

A few things to bear in mind: Not everyone experiences a school the same way. People can go to a "party school" and spend all of their time in the library. Others might spend most weekends at their academically rigorous institution passed out on the bathroom floor. You are very much the creator of your own college experience. Many schools appear on more than one list because there are multiple aspects to a school's personality.

Also know that reputations (and realities) change all the time. A school that's known for its Greek system could ban fraternities from campus. A school that's known for its athletics could lose a couple of championships and shift focus, while another might gain a sports following. The best way for you to get to know the personality of a school is to visit it yourself, and be aware of the omnipresent possibility for change.

The list of schools in the following sections are just a sampling of what's out there. For comprehensive listings of colleges and universities, get one of the big, fat, classic guidebooks.

SEE RESOURCES, P. 105 FOR GUIDEBOOK SUGGESTIONS

SMALL LIBERAL ARTS SCHOOLS

At a liberal arts school, the focus is on intellectual skills, rather than professional or vocational ones. You're more likely to learn how to think critically about Russian playwrights than how to start and manage a business. Liberal arts schools are also known for smaller student bodies and high-quality teaching, focusing on student-professor interaction and small student-to-faculty ratios. Some people enjoy the intimacy of a small school, while others may find it stifling. But liberal arts colleges are really too diverse to characterize in a few sentences; suffice it to say that they range from sporty to religious, from urban to rural, from incredibly selective to come-one-come-all.

SOME WELL-KNOWN LIBERAL ARTS SCHOOLS

Amherst College (Amherst, MA)
Barnard College (New York, NY)
Beloit College (Beloit, WI)
Bucknell University (Lewisburg, PA)
Carleton College (Northfield, MN)
Claremont McKenna College (Claremont, CA)
Colby College (Waterville, ME)
College of Wooster (Wooster, OH)
Denison University (Granville, OH)
Furman University (Greenville, SC)
Gettysburg College (Gettysburg, PA)
Hampshire College (Amherst, MA)
Haverford College (Haverford, PA)
Kalamazoo College (Kalamazoo, MI)
Macalester College (St. Paul, MN)
Reed College (Portland, OR)
Sarah Lawrence College (Bronxville, NY)
Skidmore College (Saratoga Springs, NY)
Swarthmore College (Swarthmore, PA)
Thomas More College (Crestview Hills, KY)
Vassar College (Poughkeepsie, NY)
Whitman College (Walla Walla, WA)
Williams College (Williamstown, MA)

I originally wanted a small school, but it became too small—so I am transferring to Cornell University.
(Connecticut College, New London)

My school is fairly small. The smallness allowed for closeness among students . . . Academically the school is great. I only wish that the school was more diverse.
(Canisius College, Buffalo, NY)

I LOVE the smallness and intimacy of my school. I don't have to walk far for classes, everyone is friendly, AND there are still lots of activities and opportunities. I love how it feels safe and inviting.
(Lebanon Valley College, Annville, PA)

I thought a small college would be good for me, but since I didn't like a lot of people who went there, it was hard to make friends. Also, my classes were small, but I still had teachers who didn't know my name or didn't make themselves readily available to students.
(Carlow College, Pittsburgh, PA)

When I started my college search, I knew I wanted a relatively small school with intimate, interactive classes. I also knew I wanted a liberal arts education. I thought I knew, however, that I did not want to attend Williams; the college is only thirty minutes from my house . . . However, after visiting several schools similar to Williams I realized I was looking for love in all the wrong places. I fell in love with Williams the second I stepped on campus for an official tour/interview.

It was a bit of an anomaly, but on a campus with 2,000 students, I saw and met new people on a daily basis.

You can get all the personal attention you may or may not need at Williams. The professors are extremely involved with their students. Athletic teams are an undeniable, but not overbearing presence on campus.
(Williams College)

If you're an eccentric film buff with true passion for the arts and a distaste for mathematics and sports, then Emerson is the perfect school for you. Emerson's biggest major is film studies, followed by television production, acting, creative writing, animation, and journalism. Students declare a major before arriving at school; most of us have known for years what we wanted to study. Professors are usually industry leaders themselves—CNN correspondents, **Boston Globe** reporters, professional actors—with an anything-goes approach to final projects that encourages students to tap into their creativity.
(Emerson College, Boston, MA)

I knew I would rather go to a smaller school where I could have a more intimate relationship with my teachers and classmates. The area is nice, but there is really nothing to do in the town.
(Vassar College)

I think you make a lot MORE friends at a small school because you end up seeing everyone pretty often whereas at a big school people get lost in the crowd. For variety, I did a semester at U.C. Berkeley which was eye-opening with its vast array of classes and people.
(Swarthmore College)

I know it sounds kind of vain, but I didn't know if I could handle going from being a well-known "star student" in my small town to being a nobody at a big university. My college still has lots of opportunities for me to expand my horizons and experience diversity, but there's also a measure of security.
(Central College, Pella, IA)

Skidmore is the perfect size for a student worried about feeling overwhelmed or lost at a larger university. The student-faculty ratio is 11 to 1, so there is plenty of attention from professors, and lively classroom discussions are almost guaranteed.
(Skidmore College)

BIG STATE UNIVERSITIES

A wide range of scholastic and social opportunities are among the many attractions of large public universities like these. In big schools, you can almost always find someone (or, more likely, a group of people) with similar interests. Some people enjoy the anonymity of a huge student population. Many students find ways to make it feel more intimate—by becoming part of a smaller community like a sorority or club, for instance. You may also have to work harder to tailor an academic program that suits your needs. State schools are usually less expensive than private ones, especially if you're in-state. Because of this, there's sometimes not much geographical diversity.

POPULAR BIG STATE SCHOOLS

Arizona State University (Tempe)
Indiana University (Bloomington)
Michigan State University (East Lansing)
Ohio State University (Columbus)
Pennsylvania State University (State College)
Texas A&M University (College Station)
University of Florida (Gainesville)
University of Michigan (Ann Arbor)
University of Minnesota (Minneapolis)
University of Texas (Austin)
University of Wisconsin (Madison)

The biggest state school is the University of Texas at Austin, with 52,261 students.

Since I was from a big city, it just felt right going to a big or medium-sized school.
(Michigan State University)

Nothing to do at all if you don't like sports, Greek life, or drinking.
(Pennsylvania State University)

I wanted to go to a big school and have all the college opportunities of a big college. I wanted to be in a sorority and participate in all the fun big college activities. I really didn't want to go to a small private school and miss out on the dorm life and all that fun stuff . . . I love the people. I love my sorority. I love the big campus life.
(University of California, Los Angeles)

If my school is known as the "Ivy League" of state schools, I think it lives up to its reputation. It is pretty academically competitive. We have students who have the same SAT scores as Ivy Leaguers, and the classes are definitely not a piece of a cake.
(State University of New York, Binghamton)

I wanted to go somewhere big and diverse, and I love how EVERYONE seems like they have school spirit. I LOVE how there's something for everyone. There are sooooo many opportunities for involvement and choices for everything. No one is left out unless they choose to be.
(Ohio State University)

There are a lot of people who attend ISU, so more activities are offered. In addition, you don't have to worry that everyone will know you are a freshman on campus, because generally people don't even notice.
(Illinois State University, Normal)

I love the diversity here. I don't feel like as much of an outcast.
(Wayne State University, Detroit, MI)

Unlike some large state schools, Rutgers is made up of many smaller colleges. While all University students take classes together, students are required to choose a college affiliation and seem to get the best of both worlds: big university resources plus personal attention. Rutgers understands that the whole college experience is overwhelming and that it's easy for students to get lost. The colleges, with various organizations all their own, offer something for everyone; the key is to get out there and explore!
(Rutgers University, New Brunswick, NJ)

At first, I wasn't really into going to a "state school"—I really wanted to travel out of state (far from my parents). I almost didn't go because of the size, but I'm glad I did go, because I have so many opportunities and resources . . .
(University of Maryland, College Park)

I like the big school because I went to a big high school. I chose my school for my major because it is ranked third in the nation, but the size also helped.
(Middle Tennessee State University, Mufreesboro)

THE **BEST** OF THE BIGGEST

The following state schools have excellent reputations and, as a result, attract lots of out-of-state residents:

University of California (Berkeley)
University of California (San Diego)
University of Illinois (Urbana-Champaign)
University of Maryland (College Park)
University of Michigan (Ann Arbor)
University of North Carolina (Chapel Hill)
University of Virginia (Charlottesville)
University of Wisconsin (Madison)

SPORTS SCHOOLS

At sports schools, athletes are stars (and sometimes do go on to be real sports stars). Much of the social life revolves around sporting events, so if cheering on the home team is your idea of fun (and you don't mind the near-constant pa-rum-pa-pa-rum of a practicing marching band), you might want to consider the following schools that place a strong emphasis on sports. Private schools, big state schools, and small liberal arts schools can all be sports schools.

SOME SCHOOLS WITH STRONG SPORTS PROGRAMS

Boston College (Chestnut Hill, MA)
Clemson University (Clemson, SC)
Duke University (Durham, NC)
Florida State University (Tallahassee)
Iowa State University (Ames)
Kansas State University (Manhattan)
Mississippi State University (Mississippi State)
Ohio State University (Columbus)
Oregon State University (Corvallis)
Pennsylvania State University (University Park)
Purdue University (West Lafayette, IN)
Seton Hall University (South Orange, NJ)
Texas A&M University (College Station)
United States Naval Academy (Annapolis, MD)
University of Alabama (Tuscaloosa)
University of Connecticut (Storrs)
University of Georgia (Athens)
University of North Carolina (Chapel Hill)
University of Notre Dame (Notre Dame, IN)
University of Tennessee (Knoxville)

Until about ten years ago, some athletes from the University of Florida in Gainesville lived in a dorm that was actually inside the football stadium. To this day, athletes there have special gyms, dining halls, even advising centers. And they get to pick their classes before anyone else.

My school reputation compares well to my experience. My school is known for hard workers and students who achieve the standard. I do just that. Plus, my school is known for its great sports program, and although I don't participate in it, I'm always at the games supporting my school!

(Providence College, RI)

I grew up in a very political scene. Many of my classmates wanted to be involved in politics, but I didn't. So because this school didn't focus on politics much, I enjoyed it and it was my first pick . . . The athletic program is great. We have good teams, great fans, and it's just all-around good.
(University of Wisconsin, Platteville)

I would say it is an all-around school. I mean, we have a really good sports program and a wonderful academic program. Those two things don't often go hand in hand in college. Most schools with good sports teams aren't known for their academics and, well, you never hear about Harvard's amazing basketball season.
(University of North Carolina)

Before attending UNLV, all I heard about the school was the sporting events. I'm not the sporty type, so I've basically just learned that there's a lot more to this school than just sports . . . I hate feeling stressed or not getting something. I hate that it's so concerned with sports, when the art department struggles at times or is not recognized.
(University of Las Vegas, NV)

Oh, man! Never come around on the OSU vs. Michigan game weekend!!!!! I want to see the game really bad, but I watch it on TV from home because there's no way I'll even be up there. There're always riots and whatnot.
(Ohio State University)

THE **BEST** COLLEGES FOR WOMEN ATHLETES*

Abilene Christian University (Abilene, TX)
Bloomsburg University (PA)
College of New Jersey (Ewing)
Penn State (State College, PA)
Princeton University (Princeton, NJ)
Stanford University (Palo Alto, CA)
Trinity University (San Antonio, TX)
University of Arizona (Tuscon)
University of California (Davis)
University of Florida (Gainesville)
University of Georgia (Athens)
University of Maryland (College Park)
University of North Carolina (Chapel Hill)
University of Texas (Austin)
Williams College (Williamstown, MA)

*ACCORDING TO SPORTS ILLUSTRATED FOR WOMEN

PARTY SCHOOLS

Reputed "party schools" are places best known for playing hard. For students who like to put studying on the back burner come Thursday night, the following schools offer a notoriously feisty social life:

SOME HARD-PARTYING SCHOOLS

Albion College (Albion, MI)
Arizona State University (Tempe)
DePauw University (Greencastle, IN)
Florida State University (Tallahassee)
Indiana University (Bloomington)
Iowa State University (Ames)
Michigan State University (East Lansing)
Ohio Wesleyan University (Delaware)
Saint Bonaventure University (Saint Bonaventure, NY)
San Jose State University (CA)
Syracuse University (Syracuse, NY)
Tulane University (New Orleans, LA)
University of Alabama (Tuscaloosa)
University of Arizona (Tucson)
University of Colorado (Boulder)
University of Dayton (Dayton, OH)
University of Florida (Gainesville)
University of Georgia (Athens)
University of Illinois (Urbana-Champaign)
University of Michigan (Ann Arbor)
University of Mississippi (Oxford)
University of North Carolina (Chapel Hill)
University of the South (Sewanee, TN)
University of Texas (Austin)
Wake Forest University (Winston-Salem, NC)
Washington and Lee University (Lexington, VA)

Playboy compiles an annual list of party schools based on beer consumption, drug use, and number of arrests per year at parties.

I know my school isn't known for it's great academics, it's more known for it's parties. But that is okay with me, because I know that I like it here and I am learning.
(Southern Illinois University, Carbondale)

MSU is a known party school, but I haven't really been to that many parties, so it hasn't really jaded my experience. It's a mix between partying and studying; you just have to learn to balance.
(Michigan State University)

I heard it was a big party school, and my first week I couldn't believe how much of an understatement "big party scene school" was!
(Boston College, Chestnut Hill, MA)

The school has a "party" school reputation. But it's what you do that makes your college experience, not how your school is.
(Georgia Southern University, Statesboro)

GREEK-HEAVY SCHOOLS

"Greek" schools often correspond with party schools—but fraternities and sororities do more than drink. The idea behind Greek organizations is one of social support and community service. At Greek-heavy schools, fraternities and sororities throw a lot of the parties on campus and have a decisive influence on the tone of social life. At some places Greek life can be hard to get away from (at the University of the South, for instance, almost 90 percent of students are involved in sororities and fraternities), but at others, Greek organizations just exist; they don't take over campus social life.

SOME SCHOOLS WITH AN ACTIVE GREEK LIFE

Birmingham-Southern College (AL)
Centre College (Danville, KY)
College of William and Mary (Williamsburg, VA)
Dartmouth College (Hanover, NH)
DePauw University (Greencastle, IN)
Emory University (Atlanta, GA)
Lehigh University (Bethlehem, PA)
Massachusetts Institute of Technology (Cambridge)
Northwestern University (Evanston, IL)
Rhodes College (Memphis, TN)
Texas Christian University (Fort Worth)
Union College (Schenectady, NY)
University of Illinois (Urbana-Champaign)
University of Redlands (Redlands, CA)
University of the South (Sewanee, TN)
Wake Forest University (Winston-Salem, NC)
Washington and Lee University (Lexington, VA)
Whitman College (Walla Walla, WA)
Wofford College (Spartanburg, SC)

Sorority girls, on average, have higher GPAs than non-Greek girls. But more of them qualify as binge drinkers, too.

IVY LEAGUE/SEVEN SISTERS

The Ivy League is known largely for its reputation. These private schools are old, prestigious, extremely selective, and academically rigorous. But each Ivy is different: Brown University in Rhode Island has a long tradition of artsy, left-leaning students; Dartmouth, in New Hampshire, is known for its Greek scene and bad weather; and Cornell, in New York, has a beautiful rural campus.

THE IVIES

Brown University (Providence, RI)
Columbia University (New York, NY)
Cornell University (Ithaca, NY)
Dartmouth College (Hanover, NH)
Harvard University (Cambridge, MA)
Princeton University (Princeton, NJ)
Yale University (New Haven, CT)
University of Pennsylvania (Philadelphia, PA)

THE SEVEN SISTERS

Barnard College (New York, NY)
Bryn Mawr College (Bryn Mawr, PA)
Mount Holyoke College (South Hadley, MA)
Smith College (Northampton, MA)
Vassar College (Poughkeepsie, NY)
Wellesley College (Wellesley, MA)

The Ivy League began as a football league for prestigious men's colleges that were close enough to play one another (which explains the concentration of Ivies in the Northeast).

The Seven Sisters were originally a group of all-female sister schools, associated with the Ivies. Although the Ivy League schools are coed now, most of the Seven Sisters are still women's schools (with the exception of Vassar, which started admitting men in 1969, and Radcliffe, which was subsumed into Harvard in 1999).

No matter what kind of person you are, you can find a group of people who can relate to you.
(Harvard University)

The colleges that appealed to me were seemingly "well-rounded"—that is, had strong academic and extracurricular activities, offered a real college experience. I also wanted to have a college that had a program in design or architecture, in which I thought I might be interested in majoring. Penn seemed to have it all—well respected with great academics, social atmosphere, and college campus (ivy walls and all); plus, it was near big cities to explore on the East Coast. Penn is first-rate: challenging, exciting, spirited . . . invaluable experiences in and out of the classroom. I loved the intellectual setting—being surrounded by well-rounded and bright classmates and teachers.

(University of Pennsylvania)

It's weird, but special. It is one of the oddest but also the most supportive possible places. People play "quiddich" on the lawn and carry around lanterns, but I have made incredible friendships. Students at Bryn Mawr are generally very ambitious, very kind, and very interesting.

(Bryn Mawr College)

I decided to apply to colleges that seemed to have a philosophy similar to my own, allowed me to make many curriculum decisions for myself, were neither huge (like Cornell) nor tiny and remote (like Bates), and which gave me a good feeling upon visiting them. Brown was my top choice from the start. Brown has an open curriculum, which gives students a lot of freedom (perhaps too much) to choose what courses to take. I like the student activism. It's academically rigorous without being snobby . . . I love all of the options in terms of extracurriculars and volunteer/community service opportunities.

(Brown University)

With just over five thousand students (not to mention the obvious oodles of money), Yale has enough facilities to keep most people happy and interested, but not so many people that it's impossible to find someone you get along with. Although the college system is supposed to be calculated to help students find companionship, I met most of the people I talk to through the freshman core humanities program (Directed Studies) or through the Jewish community . . . Since it's clearly a killer idea to go through many of the major texts of Western Civilization in small groups of interested students, if you get good teachers your freshman year has a lot of potential.

(Yale University)

Most people buy into the Cornell University myth of snow, suicide and studying. But they should also know that it is one of the best schools in the world—a school where beloved children's author E.B. White, Supreme Court Justice Ruth Bader Ginsburg, and ice cream kings Ben and Jerry started their famous careers—as students. As for suicides, a majority of Cornell students are happy campers. They take courses in practical subjects such as electrical engineering, history, and biology, but also in winemaking and beekeeping. Cornell probably has the best dining hall food in the country. Who can complain when there's gourmet New York cheesecake and daily chef's specials? . . . If you come to learn, you will learn more than you ever imagined. You will also certainly gain a lot more weight than you want to.

(Cornell University)

For lack of a better cliché, the Princeton faculty is topnotch. Classes are small in size and held in every conceivable topic . . . Social life is another matter. The town of Princeton is by no means a bustling metropolis, and in-town activities are extremely limited. To remedy this, most of the student body turns to Thursday and Saturday night free-for-alls involving cheap beer and random hook-ups out at the "Street." Ah, the Street (literally a street), home to a series of "eating clubs"—mansions in which upperclassmen eat their meals and attend weekend parties—that propagate an elitist system of membership into which most students get sucked.

(Princeton University)

GREAT TECH SCHOOLS

"Tech" schools emphasize education and career training in technical fields, like engineering, science, or math. They're often reputed for their graduate research facilities, and for undergrads they usually offer liberal arts courses to supplement the technical ones. Since many of these schools attract fewer women, there is often plenty of financial aid available for those who are admitted. If you have the skills in these areas, check out these schools.

FAMOUS TECHNICAL INSTITUTES

California Institute of Technology (Pasadena)
California Polytechnic State University (San Luis Obispo)
Georgia Institute of Technology (Atlanta)
Harvey Mudd College (Claremont, CA)
Massachusetts Institute of Technology (Cambridge)
Rensselaer Polytechnic Institute (Troy, NY)
Rochester Institute of Technology (Rochester, NY)
Rose-Hulman Institute of Technology (Terre Haute, IN)
Virginia Polytechnic Institute and State University (Blacksburg)

ULTRA-INTELLECTUAL SCHOOLS

These schools have unusually intense admissions and academic requirements—and unusually bright student populations:

SOME INTELLIGENTSIA FAVORITES

Carleton College (Northfield, MN)
Carnegie Mellon University (Pittsburgh, PA)
Case Western Reserve University (Cleveland, OH)
Johns Hopkins University (Baltimore, MD)
Massachusetts Institute of Technology (Cambridge)
Rice University (Houston, TX)
Stanford University (Palo Alto, CA)
Swarthmore College (Swarthmore, PA)
University of Chicago (IL)

I think what I love about the school is that in spite of its top-ranking schools of business, computer science and engineering; its excellence in the sciences, drama, music, art, cognitive science, psychology, philosophy and many other fields; and the fact that it practically created the field of robotics, Carnegie Mellon is able to sit back and enjoy the lighter side. This attitude is reflected in humorous newspapers such as the readme, as well as in daily student life: Most CMU students can laugh at themselves—and we can ALL laugh at the computer science majors.

(Carnegie Mellon University)

I always loved characters and stories. I wanted to be a cartoonist when I was eight years old. I used to draw figures all the time and make animations. I worked for *Time* magazine for a summer during college as a photojournalist too, but that didn't really express what I wanted.

When I was finishing up at the University of Chicago, I went to one of my favorite professors to talk about what I should do next. She said, "Well, you obviously want to be a filmmaker." I said, "I do?" She said, "Yeah, it's all you ever talk about." I applied to film school after that.

KIMBERLY PEIRCE, FILMMAKER

HOW I GOT HERE

URBAN SCHOOLS

City schools usually have the advantage of a diverse population and lots of cultural stimulation outside of campus life. However, stimulation can also be distracting, and, in some cities, safety is a real issue.

I love being in the city. But my campus is a little on the suburban side, which helps me not get too distracted by city life. (University of Toronto, Ontario, Canada)

FOR MORE ON SAFETY, SEE P. 88.

SOME FUN CITY SCHOOLS

American University (Washington, DC)
Boston University (MA)
Columbia University (New York, NY)
George Washington University (Washington, DC)
Johns Hopkins University (Baltimore, MD)
New York University (New York)
University of California (Los Angeles)
University of Chicago (IL)
University of Houston (TX)
University of Pennsylvania (Philadelphia)

GREAT COLLEGE TOWNS

Ann Arbor, MI (University of Michigan)
Athens, GA (University of Georgia)
Austin, TX (University of Texas at Austin)
Boston, MA (Boston University, Boston College, Northeastern University, Emerson College, University of Massachusetts in Boston)
Boulder, CO (University of Colorado at Boulder)
Charlottesville, VA (University of Virginia)
Hanover, NH (Dartmouth College)
Madison, WI (University of Wisconsin at Madison)
Minneapolis, MN (University of Minnesota, Minneapolis College of Art and Design, Walden University)
Princeton, NJ
    (Princeton University)

New York University (NYU) is located in the heart of New York City's Greenwich Village, and students are reminded of that at every turn. The school's "un-campus" (as students call it) is a series of brownstone buildings. NYU has practically colonized historic Washington Square, using the perimeter of the park as a mini-campus "quad" for students and faculty alike. Most NYU students prefer to get their entertainment from the city itself, relying on local nightlife and art galleries that are in turn fairly receptive to what NYU students have to offer. For students who can handle the noise of the big city and the compounded pressures of college life and subway commutes, NYU is the place to be. All urban campuses blend into their cities somehow, but NYU is especially good at being PART of New York City.
(New York University)

The urban and diversity part affected me in that I come from an urban, diverse area. Naturally, I would feel most comfortable in a setting that I'm already familiar with. (Fairleigh Dickinson University, Teaneck, NJ)

I like my city. Lately, the indie scene has been growing. Lots of concerts, little coffee houses, art shows, things a college kid can enjoy.
(University of Las Vegas, NV)

If you're bored, hop on the subway. If you're bored after you reach your destination, it's your fault, not NYC's.
(City University of New York, Brooklyn)

CULTURALLY DIVERSE SCHOOLS

With any school you're researching, you'll be able to find statistics regarding the diversity of its students. The following schools have a higher-than-average mix of student ethnicities.

SOME MELTING-POT SCHOOLS

Barnard College (New York, NY)
City University of New York (CUNY) (New York, NY)
Emory University (Atlanta, GA)
Harvard University (Cambridge, MA)
Johns Hopkins University (Baltimore, MD)
New York University (New York)
Occidental College (Los Angeles, CA)
Rutgers University (NJ)
University of California (Berkeley)
University of Houston (TX)
Yale University (New Haven, CT)

On my freshman floor, I lived with four students from other countries, a few classmates who could commute home every weekend, and others from all over the United States. As a collective, we could have checked off every race on a typical questionnaire. As for religious diversity, I didn't have to go beyond my floor to talk to Islamic, Hindi, Jewish or Christian students.
(Columbia University)

The number one thing I loved about attending SUNY Albany was its diversity. Not only does the mood encourage individuality, but the school is unusually tolerant of difference—sometimes even seeming to yearn for it. Every cause, every issue, has a group representing it. This could make for a segregation problem, but at Albany, there is a remarkable feeling of unity.
(State University of New York, Albany)

I think I liked the anonymity in going to a large school. I wanted to get away from the cliquishness of high school. I always felt that suffocated me, kept me from growing. So I went to college in the city, a place where I could explore a new, different life and specifically feel comfortable (and not in the spotlight) being gay.
(New York University)

Although females are still a minority here, there is a good level of political diversity and a large gay population. Activities range from political activism to performance groups to "just-for-fun" clubs, and students can be as active or isolated as they choose.
(Carnegie Mellon University, Pittsburgh, PA)

RURAL SCHOOLS

In addition to offering a peaceful, bucolic setting, rural schools generally foster a strong sense of community because students stay on campus more.

SOME COLLEGES IN THE COUNTRY

Bard College (Annandale-on-Hudson, NY)
Berea College (Berea, KY)
Colgate University (Hamilton, NY)
College of the Ozarks (Point Lookout, MO)
Emmanuel College (Franklin Springs, GA)
Hamilton College (Clinton, NY)
Lincoln University (Lincoln University, PA)
Oberlin College (Oberlin, OH)
Rust College (Holly Springs, MS)
Slippery Rock University of Pennsylvania
    (Slippery Rock)
University of West Alabama (Livingston)
Washington and Lee University (Lexington, VA)
Webber International University (Babson Park, FL)
Williams College (Williamstown, MA)

The campus is definitely in the middle of nowhere, but I liked that. Williams is a strong community, and I believe its location plays an important role in that; because Williams isn't in a bustling metropolis or surrounded by four other colleges, people stay on campus for the weekends, and that's very nice.
(Williams College)

I LOVE the quietness at night and being able to study . . .
(University of Illinois, Urbana-Champaign)

Living in a big city, I wanted to go somewhere quieter and more "outdoorsy." We're not exactly in the backwoods, but it's pretty.
(Middlebury College)

I guess we are different from other colleges because we have more environmentally based majors (landscape architecture, architecture, pre-vet, soil science, etc.) . Our campus is beautiful, with hills scattered with Arabian horses, cows, pigs, sheep, etc. I would have to say that most of the students I see don't care about fashion and materialistic things.
(California State Polytechnic University, Pomona)

BEAUTIFUL CAMPUSES
Arizona State University (Tempe)
California Polytechnic State University (Pomona)
Cornell University (Ithaca, NY)
Elon University (Elon, NC)
Humboldt State University (Arcata, CA)
Indiana University (Bloomington, IN)
Mary Washington College (Fredericksburg, VA)
Mount Holyoke College (South Hadley, MA)
Pepperdine University (Malibu, CA)
Princeton University (Princeton, NJ)
Rhodes College (Memphis, TN)
University of California (Santa Cruz)
University of Colorado (Boulder)
University of Kansas (Lawrence)
University of Miami (FL)
University of North Carolina (Chapel Hill)
University of Richmond (VA)
University of Washington (Seattle)
Wagner College (Staten Island, NY)

> The campus is absolutely beautiful. It's all woods with a pond running through it and lots of hills, which isn't so fun in the winter.
> (Augustana College, Rock Island, IL)

TOP OUTDOORS SCHOOLS*
Bowdoin College (Brunswick, ME)
Colorado College (Colorado Springs)
Cornell University (Ithaca, NY)
Dartmouth College (Hanover, NH)
Humboldt State University (Arcata, CA)
Middlebury College (Middlebury, VT)
Montana State University (Bozeman)
Northern Arizona University (Flagstaff)
Simon Fraser University (British Columbia)
Southern Oregon University (Ashland)
Stanford University (Palo Alto, CA)
University of California (Santa Cruz)
University of Colorado (Boulder)
University of Hawaii (Hilo)
University of Iowa (Iowa City)
University of Montana (Missoula)
University of Vermont (Burlington)
University of Virginia (Charlottesville)
University of Wisconsin (Madison)
Warren Wilson College (Asheville, NC)

> Much of the time, students can take a break from the books and enjoy Cornell's green and gorgeous landscape. Here, you can go jogging among some of the most scenic trails in the Northeast. You can picnic in Slim Jim Woods and hear owls calling in the dark by Fall Creek. You can be struggling over a problem set in Mann Library, look out into a thick canopy of leaves, and suddenly feel that everything will be fine.
> (Cornell University)

*ACCORDING TO **OUTSIDE MAGAZINE**

CRUNCHY/ARTSY/PROGRESSIVE SCHOOLS

Students looking for academic freedom—and the responsibility that comes with it—will enjoy these schools offering alternative grading systems, course offerings, and/or academic schedules. At many of these schools, adamantly organic food, impromptu campus-quad drum circles, and the inimitable waft of patchouli are all familiar features. Others offer dual-purpose learning—earning a bachelor's degree and acquiring professional training in a specific field of design or the arts.

SOME CREATIVE SCHOOLS

Antioch College (Yellow Springs, OH)
Bard College (Annandale-on-Hudson, NY)
Bennington College (Bennington, VT)
Brown University (Providence, RI)
California College of Arts and Crafts (San Francisco)
California Institute of the Arts (Valencia)
Colorado College (Colorado Springs)
Earlham College (Richmond, IN)
Evergreen State College (Olympia, WA)
Grinnell College (Grinnell, IA)
Guilford College (Greensboro, NC)
Hampshire College (Amherst, MA)
Howard University (Washington, DC)
Lewis and Clark College (Portland, OR)
Macalester College (Saint Paul, MN)
New College of Florida (Sarasota)
Eugene Lang College of New School University (New York, NY)
North Carolina School of the Arts (Winston-Salem)
Oberlin College (Oberlin, OH)
Reed College (Portland, OR)
Sarah Lawrence College (Bronxville, NY)
School of the Art Institute of Chicago (IL)
Simon's Rock College of Bard (Great Barrington, MA)
Skidmore College (Saratoga Springs, NY)
University of California (Berkeley)
University of California (Santa Cruz)
University of Oregon (Eugene)
University of Puget Sound (Tacoma, WA)
University of Wisconsin (Madison)
Vassar College (Poughkeepsie, NY)
Wesleyan University (Middletown, CT)
Whitman College (Walla Walla, WA)

FOR MORE INFORMATION ON FINE ARTS SCHOOLS, SEE P. 112.

The best words to describe both the college and the student body would have to be "political" and "creative." "Tiny" would probably come in third, as there are only about 500 students and full-time faculty are very few. Although Lang boasts that it welcomes students of all political beliefs, you probably won't find that to be true in the classroom. Most Lang students are aligned with one or more progressive causes, and more attention is paid in the curriculum to marginalized voices than at most schools. (Eugene Lang College of New School University, New York, NY)

It is very accepting and supportive of its gay community (rare in Arkansas), and I have made some incredible friends. Plus, there are recycling receptacles in all the dorm corridors. (Hendrix College, Conway, AR)

ACTIVISM

For many people, college is a time to really explore and act on political beliefs. College students are often at the forefront of progressive political movements. In fact, student uprisings have changed the course of history in some countries!

On your own for the first time and given the freedom and resources to think independently, college is a natural time to come into your political self. You're also part of a community where it's very likely that you will find others who share your beliefs and your passion for a particular issue—whether it's a broad issue like environmentalism or animal rights, or something more focused, like the plight of Iraqi women.

Whether you join a club, volunteer with a local or national organization, or launch your own on-campus movement or protest, activism can expand your mind and your social circle.

I had a lot of strong opinions about unequal treatment of different kinds of people, ranging from how students were being treated in [high] school to the civil rights movement. I remember wishing that we had spent more time on Martin Luther King Jr. in history class.

I was a cultural anthropology major in college. One of the principles of cultural anthropology fieldwork was not to interfere with what you see. I started to become very frustrated with that idea by the end of college. I wanted to make changes. I didn't want to sit by the sidelines and just watch, so I decided that law school was the way to go. In college, I became a political activist. American foreign policy in Central America, campus issues, and reproductive freedom in particular drew my attention. By the end of college, I knew I was leaning toward civil rights generally and wanted to make changes. Then I came out as a lesbian. So that was the final confirmation, and ultimately led me to do the kind of work that I'm doing now.

LESLIE COOPER,
LAWYER WITH THE
AMERICAN CIVIL
LIBERTIES UNION
(ACLU)

HOW I GOT HERE

My father was in the magazine publishing business, so we had a lot of magazines around the house. Although I wasn't really looking at them from a critical viewpoint consciously, I think they influenced me. I modeled in high school and became aware of the kind of power that beauty seems to give young women, but also of the drawbacks. I was also involved in drama and debating, which gave me a good foundation for a career in public speaking.

After college, I had a job putting ads into a medical journal. I was shocked by an ad for birth control pills that featured a smiling woman's head and the caption "Ovulen 21 works the way a woman thinks—by weekdays not by cycle days." Inside the woman's head were seven boxes, one for each day of the week, and inside each box was a picture of each day's activity—Monday had a laundry basket, Tuesday an iron, etc. That is the first ad I looked at and thought, "There is really something wrong here." From that point on I collected ads and examined what they said about what it means to be a woman in this society.

DR. JEAN KILBOURNE, MEDIA CRITIC AND ACTIVIST

HOW I GOT HERE

MILITARY SCHOOLS

Military schools have a lot to offer:
They're usually free, there's 100 percent job placement, and if you're considering a career in the military, they'll give you a great step up. But they're also hard work, and don't forget—if the military pays for your schooling, you owe them several years of your life.

The Citadel (Charleston, SC)
US Air Force Academy (Colorado Springs, CO)
US Coast Guard Academy (New London, CT)
US Merchant Marines Academy (Kings Point, NY)
US Military Academy (West Point, NY)
US Naval Academy (Annapolis, MD)

I received a full scholarship from Air Force ROTC. I liked going to boot camp, in general, and I liked the classroom experience. I did think that some of the classes were a little contrived and boring, and I did think that some of the students as ROTC cadets took their "rank" a little more seriously than they should. (In other words, I didn't like having to call someone sir/ma'am who was in my class, but a cadet lieutenant colonel, while I was cadet lieutenant. I thought it was degrading and didn't add anything to my military discipline.)
(College of Saint Scholastica, Duluth, MN)

- Class rings were invented at West Point, and have since spread to almost every high school and college in the country.

- Freshmen at West Point, called "plebes," must be able to summarize every article on the front page of the *New York Times* if an upperclassman asks them. They also have to recite the daily mess hall menu on command.

- In 1993, Shannon Faulkner applied to the Citadel and deleted all reference of her gender on the application. She was accepted, but when the school found out she was a girl, they withdrew their acceptance. She took them to court and won. She dropped out pretty soon after enrolling in 1996 (due to heavy sentiment against her on campus), but she paved the way for women at other military academies.

FOR INFO ON JOINING THE MILITARY, SEE P. 146. FOR INFO ON ROTC, SEE P. 147.

FOCUSED-POPULATION SCHOOLS

Some people prefer to be in a school where the student population, at least on the surface, resembles them most. For some, it gives them a level of comfort; for others, it minimizes distractions.

WOMEN'S SCHOOLS

Studies show that women who attend single-sex colleges participate more fully inside and outside the classroom, and that they excel in traditionally masculine fields more than their coed counterparts.

SOME WOMEN-ONLY SCHOOLS

Agnes Scott College (Decatur, GA)
Barnard College (New York, NY)
Bryn Mawr College (PA)
Hollins University (Roanoke, VA)
Mills College (Oakland, CA)
Mount Holyoke College (South Hadley, MA)
Randolph-Macon Woman's College
    (Lynchburg, VA)
Scripps College (Claremont, CA)
Simmons College (Boston, MA)
Smith College (Northampton, MA)
Spelman College (Atlanta, GA)
Sweet Briar College (Sweet Briar, VA)
Trinity College (Hartford, CT)
Wellesley College (Wellesley, MA)
Wells College (Aurora, NY)

I both love and hate the fact that Bryn Mawr is a women's college. The social scene is totally bizarre, and people spend way too much time studying (even on Saturday afternoons). However, the place would just not make sense if it were coed. Don't underestimate the importance of being able to show up for lectures in pajamas!
(Bryn Mawr College)

The variety of activities, the intense academic workload, and the constant socialization within are the best and worst parts of Smith; it's extremely easy to feel overwhelmed. Smith is definitely not for everyone, but it provides a wonderful environment for people who can handle the challenge.
(Smith College)

I really love how closely connected my school is. I am close to all of my professors, and my university's president even has a weekly open-door session during which time she invites any student who has something on her mind concerning the school to have time to discuss it with her—one on one.
(Mississippi University for Women)

BLACK SCHOOLS

Historically black colleges and universities (called HBCUs) provide unusual opportunities in higher learning, offering supportive environments for people interested in more than just their classes. People who attend HBCUs often report a greater sense of identification with their cultural background.

Alabama A&M University (Huntsville)
Alabama State University (Montgomery)
Alcorn State University (Alcorn, MS)
Barber-Scotia College (Concord, NC)
Benedict College (Columbia, SC)
Dillard University (New Orleans, LA)
Bowie State University (Bowie, MD)
Howard University (Washington, DC)
Lincoln University (Jefferson City, MO)
Fisk University (Nashville, TN)
Spelman College (Atlanta, GA)
Tuskegee University (Tuskegee, AL)
Wilberforce University (Wilberforce, OH)

HOW I GOT HERE

I ended up going to a historically black college because I wanted to major in theater. And I didn't want to be relegated to playing black roles in a white university . . . It was a wonderful experience.
RUTH SIMMONS, PRESIDENT OF BROWN UNIVERSITY

HISPANIC SCHOOLS

Hispanic Serving Institutions are colleges where at least 25 percent of enrolled students are Hispanic. These are just some examples.

Arizona Western College (Yuma)
Barry University (Miami Shores, FL)
John Jay College of Criminal Justice (New York, NY)
Donnelly College (Kansas City, KS)
Heritage College (Toppenish, WA)
MacCormac College (Chicago, IL)
Midland College (Midland, TX)
New Mexico State University (Las Cruces)
Northeastern Illinois University (Chicago)
Occidental College (Los Angeles, CA)
Phoenix College (AZ)
Saint Peter's College (Jersey City, NJ)
Santa Monica College (CA)
University of Miami (FL)
University of Texas (El Paso and San Antonio)

NATIVE AMERICAN SCHOOLS

While these schools welcome people of all backgrounds, they were established primarily for Native American students. Often located on reservations, many of these universities were started by individual tribes. They provide a postsecondary education for Native Americans who might not attend college otherwise.

Haskell Indian Nations University (Lawrence, KS)
Northwest Indian College (Bellingham, WA)
Sinte Gleska University (Mission, SD)

Every class at Wheaton College begins with a prayer or devotional, and chapel attendance is mandatory three times a week.

RELIGIOUSLY-AFFILIATED SCHOOLS

These schools pride themselves on offering a spiritual education as well as an intellectual one. To varying degrees, the philosophy and canonical literature of a specific faith influence social and academic life—in short, the total college experience—at the following schools.

PROTESTANT

Wheaton College (Wheaton, IL)
Concordia College (Bronxville, NY)

CATHOLIC

Assumption College (Worcester, MA)
Thomas Aquinas College (Santa Paula, CA)

JEWISH

Yeshiva University (New York, NY)
Baltimore Hebrew University (MD)

MORMON

Brigham Young University (Salt Lake City, UT; Laie, HI; Rexburg, ID)

BUDDHIST

Naropa University (Boulder, CO)

I am Mormon, so I chose to go there because there are people who can help me stay strong in my faith. The school is also in good academic standing. Having people of the same faith makes me more comfortable.
(Brigham Young University)

I am Lutheran and almost didn't want to go to a church-affiliated school because I didn't think they'd know how to have fun . . . but I was very wrong!
(Augustana College, Rock Island, IL)

I wanted to attend a Christian university and also a school that had a good history program . . . the Christian atmosphere and growing up going to camp there made me familiar with the town and campus . . . My Bible professors were awesome too. We were on a first-name basis with them and they were always there for us, twenty-four hours a day.
(Abilene Christian University, TX)

COLLEGE

Time was a great resource for me. I know a lot of people don't want to take the time to fill out applications and read everything, but you really just have to make up your mind to do it. I set aside an hour or so every now and then to just work on applications for a little bit. I didn't get bogged down and everything got done. My parents helped me out some too.
(Lebanon Valley College, Annville, PA)

Gearing up for college can be a stressful business, but by keeping a detailed calendar of what you need to do—on a large piece of paper tacked above your desk, for example—can help you streamline the process and stay on top of important deadlines. It's possible that every school you apply to will have different application requirements, so you definitely need to find out what these are as early as you can. But bearing in mind the following general timeline can also help you understand the overall application process.

Winter/spring of junior year: Get tested, meet with your school counselor, and start touring schools. Now's the time to sign up for the SAT and the ACT, the two standardized tests most often required for college admission. This way, if you feel you'd like to improve your scores after you get your results back, you still have an opportunity to take them again during the fall of your senior year. Also, after you and your counselor have started discussing which schools you might want to apply to, it's a great idea to begin visiting colleges to see which ones stand up to your expectations and which ones just rub you the wrong way. Spring break of junior year, as well as the summer vacation between junior and senior years, are good times to visit the schools you're curious about. But if you go when school is in session, you can often get matched up with students, which will help to give you a better sense of the school. Remember that a host student can only expose you to her individual experience of the school—which will differ from others' experiences.

Early fall of senior year: Decide which schools you're going to apply to and nail down all the pertinent information on how and when to apply. In early fall, sit down with your parents and high school guidance counselor and come up with a list of schools you'd to like attend. Your final list should include some combination of schools you should have no problem getting into based on your academic record and standardized test scores (your "safety" schools), some you feel you're very likely to get into (your strong contenders), and at least one or two that might be a stretch for you to be admitted to but that you'd try for anyway (your long shots). Then, find out immediately (if you haven't already) when the admissions deadlines are for each of the schools you're interested in and request application materials. (Often both of these tasks can be accomplished at the school's Web site. You can usually request applications as early as one year in advance of when you would like to enroll.) Finally, register to take the SAT or ACT again if you'd like to try to improve your score.

Mid-fall of senior year: Make sure your transcripts are in order. Upon receiving your applications, submit the forms requiring high school transcripts and test scores to your high school's college admissions officer (who will return the forms directly to the colleges by the appropriate deadline) and submit the recommendation forms to teachers who will be writing your letters of recommendation.

Late fall of senior year: Meet your own deadlines. Most colleges set their application deadlines in midwinter. Submit your application, with any necessary essays and required admissions fees, on or before the day they're due. Check with each school to see which shipping method they prefer, and if it's mail, consider sending your documents via express, certified, or registered mail so you can track the progress of your application and make sure it arrives on time.

Spring of senior year. Most colleges let students applying by regular admission know whether or not they've been admitted on or around April 1, so here, alas, you're looking at four to five months of nail biting and hand wringing. After receiving letters of acceptance, students are usually expected to make their decisions, and let colleges know whether or not they're coming, by May 1.

EARLY DECISION

If you feel strongly attracted to one school, you can consider applying through an "early admission" or "early decision" plan, if the school offers one. These differ slightly. Early admissions programs are nonbinding and allow students to apply to other schools either by early or regular admission deadlines and even to wait until May 1 to see which other schools accept them, and with what offers of financial aid, before making a final decision. Early decision programs, on the other hand, are binding. Under these plans, students are expected to withdraw all other college applications immediately once they've been admitted to the school they applied to early decision. Because of the strictness of early decision policies, many guidance counselors caution students against applying to college in this way. The advantage of these plans is that you can have a stress-free senior year if you are, in fact, accepted to your school of choice.

FOR INFORMATION ON FINANCIAL AID AND OTHER IDEAS FOR FINANCING OR SUBSIDIZING YOUR EDUCATION, SEE PP. 167–172.

Making your application stand out

Since students can now apply online, many schools are receiving 50 percent more applications (for the same number of spots) as when students had to go through the process of sending in written requests with self-addressed stamped envelopes. More than ever, it's important to find a way to separate yourself from the pack and establish a clear picture (beyond grades and test scores) of who you are and what unique contribution you can make to the school. Naturally, there is no one-size-fits-all formula for this. But there are two very important ways that you can be certain your unique talents and character will leap off the (electronic or printed) page.

1. Make sure that the person writing your college recommendation letter knows you well. If possible, find a teacher to write your recommendation letter who's had you in class more than once and had the chance to observe your academic and social growth. When a teacher agrees to write a recommendation for you (whether or not she or he has known you since you were a mere frosh), give him or her a typed letter outlining your goals and reasons for applying to a certain school (or schools), as well as your impressions of how you worked and what you learned in this teacher's class (or classes). This will clue your teacher in to the kind of information you're including elsewhere in your application, and, ideally, enable him or her to write a recommendation that will help flatter you and flesh out the picture you're trying to convey.

2. Write an admission essay that's honest and open—a true reflection of who you are. There are other books that can help you choose an appropriate topic, refine your grammar and rhetorical skills, and avoid the worst college-application clichés (such as "How the Poor People I Saw Once on a Trip to Tennessee Taught Me I Must Do My Part to Rid the World of Ills"). But if there's one message we'd like you to take from us, it's be yourself—not someone else you think you're supposed to be. Admissions officers have beagle noses for overreaching conceits and stories spun from thin air. So if you let your true nature—however serious or playful it may be—come through in your essay, you stand a much better chance of pleasing and intriguing your reader.

FOR RESOURCES ON ESSAY WRITING, SEE P. 105.

College Admissions Anxiety

The SATs can be extremely stressful, but the best thing you can do for yourself is to prepare (whether you take a course, take sample tests online, or study some test prep books) and get a good night's sleep the night before. Also, know that even though your score may seem like it's the most important thing in the world, there are many other factors that determine what schools you'll get into.

Tensions can run really high at acceptance time (December for those applying early decision; April for regular admissions). Everyone wants to know who got in where, and because it all happens simultaneously, it's hard not to feel like you're being compared with everyone else. And lots of people feel disappointed when they don't get into their first-choice school. It's natural to feel crushed, competitive—or elated. It's also important to remember that wherever you wind up may very well be the best place for you. And if it's not, you will always have the chance to transfer to another school (24 percent of college students do transfer).

College Rankings

It's more important for you to choose a school that feels like the best match for you than to opt for the school with the "best" ranking, since rankings are very subjective and often not based on attributes that will affect you in any way. The *US News & World Report* annual feature on "America's Best Colleges," as well as many other publications and references, create all kinds of unnecessary anxiety. As Gerhard Casper, president of Stanford University (a top-ranked school) said, "Much about these rankings—particularly their specious formulas and spurious precision—is utterly misleading."

Extracurriculars

When colleges look at applications, they want to see that you did well in school—but also that you did something besides school. After-school activities, from varsity lacrosse to piano lessons, prove to the admissions committee that you have ideas and interests beyond the classroom. And admissions officers like to see that you can manage your time, that you can maintain a long-term commitment, and that you can make a meaningful contribution to nonacademic activities. Don't worry if you weren't the president of your club or if you haven't led your team to the state championships. And at the same time, don't think that being class president will make up for poor grades or an unchallenging course schedule. You can use extracurriculars to show colleges more of who you are and what you're about—just make sure they're part of a well-rounded application.

Academics

For many people—especially those leaving home for the first time—college is liberating and exhilarating. Staying up until dawn, hanging out with new friends, sleeping until noon, and wearing clothes that might have driven their parents nuts are just a few of the ways college students celebrate their independence. But in all the potentially overwhelming social excitement, it's important to remember the real reason you're in college: to learn. Students who take charge of their academic lives from the start, selecting schools and courses intelligently and developing strong study habits, get the most out of college.

FIND THE RIGHT LEARNING ENVIRONMENT FOR YOU

To choose the academic environment for you, you'll need to think about what you want study and what kind of college—big or small, academically competitive or laid-back—will help you grow the most. Your high school counselor should be able to help steer you toward a number of different colleges appropriate for your temperament and your interests. You can also research specific schools yourself by requesting information from their admissions offices. But since the schools themselves may emphasize the most positive aspects of the courses and majors they offer, you should also consult independent college guidebooks for information about class size, most popular majors, and departments with particularly strong reputations. After narrowing your search, try to visit the schools that interest you most. Talking to students, and sitting in on classes is really the best way to get the true flavor of any school.

FOR INFO ON GOOD COLLEGE GUIDES, SEE RESOURCES, P. 105.

As with any other school, there are those classes and professors that you will have to learn to like . . . If you do not like the class from the start, check your schools drop/add period and withdraw from the class making sure you have a backup course. If you are stuck in the class, make some friends and get together in a study group if the class is really hard. Get a tutor if you really need one, too.
(Millersville University, PA)

Choose Classes Carefully

Though college may seem like it's going to last forever, four years will probably fly by. Your time to learn is limited, so it's important to seek out challenging classes and professors you respect.

At many liberal arts colleges, freshman and sophomore students are required to take a selection of courses in basic subjects, such as math, English, science, history, and philosophy. Often referred to as a "core curriculum," these classes are designed to give new students a foundation of knowledge and potentially introduce them to subjects that they may decide to major in later. (At most colleges, students are required to declare their majors by junior year.)

In addition to required classes, students have the option to pick a few classes, known as "electives," in any area that interests them. Elective courses are a great way for you to expose yourself to new ideas. You should feel free to use these credits to sign up for life-expanding courses far afield of your usual interests, if that's what you want to do.

Before you register for any class, elective or required, it's important to do some research. To avoid bad teachers and dull material—which will waste your time and tuition money—try to find out what the class will cover and what the teacher's reputation is like. At larger universities, you often have to be even pickier, since large class sizes or a lack of TAs or professors can make learning very challenging. As an incoming freshman, you're likely to be assigned an academic adviser, a member of the faculty who will help you choose your classes. Your adviser, course catalogues, and fellow students who've already taken the class can all be useful sources of information. At some schools student organizations compile student evaluations of various professors—a good way of getting first-hand feedback. But it's also helpful to visit the campus department offices of the subjects you're interested in (especially if your adviser isn't well acquainted with the

Classes at Lang aren't your traditional English and Math 101s. Selections from the course catalog include Poetry as Public Act; Drugs, Youth, Sex and Society; and Dream Interpretation. When it comes to class time, don't expect to be able to just sit back; classes are seminars and participation in the discussions is expected. Also, be prepared to write a lot of papers. Traditional tests are few and far between. The biggest drawback as far as classes go is the insane registration process. Class size is capped at 15 so there's a good chance you won't get your first choice. The administration can also be a pain. Getting face time with one of the three deans can be hard and it's something that you'll need to do more than you'd expect.
(Eugene Lang College of New School University, New York, NY)

The workload for most classes is challenging, but because Smith has no core curriculum, you'll mostly be doing work you WANT to do for classes you choose to take.
(Smith College, Northampton, MA)

One drawback at Emerson is that every major, whether it be creative writing or musical theater, is secluded. The print journalism students don't have much contact with the broadcast journalism students, and so on. And everyone has the same classmates, and professors, for years. There are ways around the isolation, however. Declaring a "minor" is common, for instance. Another secret is to join as many on-campus student organizations as possible. With over 120, Emerson College has something for everyone.

(Emerson College, Boston, MA)

Students are expected to apply to a specific college and program of study (College of Arts and Sciences freshmen, for example, can apply "undecided" but must declare within two years), but hundreds transfer internally every year. In any case, all students take a core curriculum under the school-wide Morse Academic Plan (MAP). So everyone gets a good grounding in the natural and social sciences and the liberal arts, no matter how specialized their college or major.

(New York University)

PROGRESSIVE CURRICULA

Some schools have required classes, a core curriculum, or some version of a program that forces students to take a variety of basic introductory courses (e.g., history, literature, science, language) and/or is designed to ensure that students take enough classes outside of their field of study to have a relatively balanced education. There are other schools that give students the freedom to study whatever they want. Some well-known "progressive" schools are:

Bard College (Annandale-on-Hudson, NY)
Earlham College (Richmond, IN)
Evergreen State College (Olympia, WA)
Grinnell College (Grinnell, IA)
Guilford College (Greensboro, NC)
Hampshire College (Amherst, MA)
Lewis and Clark College (Portland, OR)
Macalester College (Saint Paul, MN)
New College of the University of South
    Florida (Sarasota)
New York University (NY)
Oberlin College (OH)
Reed College (Portland, OR)
Sarah Lawrence College (Bronxville, NY)
Simon's Rock College of Bard (Great
    Barrington, MA)
Skidmore College (Saratoga Springs, NY)
Swarthmore College (Swarthmore, PA)
University of California (Santa Cruz)
University of Oregon (Eugene)
Vassar College (Poughkeepsie, NY)
Wesleyan University (Middletown, CT)

Columbia's Core Curriculum consists of a series of intense and intimate seminar courses that every undergraduate at the college must take. Most Core courses are taken during the first two years, forcing students to interact with peers of different backgrounds, perspectives and intellectual interests. Because it's an experience that every Columbia student has in common, if you're ever stuck with an attractive guy in an elevator and searching for a topic of conversation, you can always ask him how he likes Plato's Republic.

The other great thing about the Core is that it incorporates one of Columbia's greatest assets: New York City. For example, one Core course called Music Humanities requires that students go to a concert (you can get student discount seats) and write a paper about it. As Columbia students get into most of New York's museums for free, Art History classes are often held in the museums themselves. Why bother looking at slides when you have the real thing a subway ride away?

(Columbia University, New York, NY)

departments and their faculty). In each department, you should be able to find syllabi for all the courses the department is offering and arrange to speak to specific instructors about their classes.

Office hours: At most schools, teachers and graduate student teaching assistants have regular office hours, when students can drop in to ask questions about their coursework, and smart students take advantage of them whenever they're feeling stumped. Talking to teachers one-on-one, though sometimes intimidating, can help you grasp complicated concepts more quickly and make you feel more confident about expressing your ideas verbally.

Shopping Around: Finally, since many colleges offer "shopping periods" at the beginning of each semester, when students are free to try out classes on a short-term basis, it's a good idea to sit in on as many classes as you can early in the semester. That way, you can get an idea of which classes and teachers you like best before officially registering. (Another advantage of dropping in on classes during the shopping period is that you may find a professor whose reading list may not knock your socks off but whose lectures are riveting. If your school allows auditing, as most do, you can sit in on that class to hear the lectures without using credits or doing the homework.)

Something that I hate and love about college at the same time, is that you get out as much as you put in. If I study for hours for a quiz, I'll do really well on it. But there isn't really any sliding by in college. Which is a HUGE difference from my high school career.

(Middle Tennessee State University, Murfreesboro)

Develop Good Study Habits

It might take you quite a while to figure out how to get into your own study groove and find what works for you as you enter a totally different academic environment. On almost any college campus, you'll find students who boast about how they barely crack books and blow off classes every week. But these people are short-changing themselves. With few exceptions, college courses are usually significantly harder than high school classes, and most students need to do their homework and attend class regularly to absorb the material they're trying to learn. Nobody is going to stay after you to make sure you are doing your assignments. You have to answer to yourself.

Procrastination is a big issue for many college students. Students who procrastinate have worse physical health (higher levels of drinking, smoking, insomnia, and stomach problems) than those who don't. Joseph Ferrari, a psychology professor at DePaul University, told Psychology Today in 2003 that some 70 percent of college students he's surveyed report academic problems with overdue papers and putting off work.

Though many students say they work better under pressure (and act as if they couldn't care less about work), oftentimes the real reason procrastinators bluff and brag about putting off work is fear of failure—they'd rather be seen as slacking off than lacking ability. But even if you've been a procrastinator in the past, it is still possible to develop strong study habits by following a few simple steps:

1. **Plan rather than cram.** Lasting learning takes place when you feed your brain new information repeatedly, rather than all at once, so try to establish a manageable short-, medium-, and long-term studying schedule for yourself.

2. **Take regular study breaks.** It can be tricky to find the right balance between studying and socializing, but research shows that relaxation is actually essential to efficient learning. If you study hard for a couple of hours, then reward yourself by meeting a friend for a sandwich, you'll probably return to your books more sharply focused than if you'd studied straight through lunch.

3. **Set realistic goals.** If the fear of failure is keeping you from trying your best in school (or trying at all), try to cultivate a more positive, accepting view of yourself. You probably won't excel in all academic areas, all the time—hardly anyone does. But if you focus on small challenges one at a time, your confidence will grow.

4. **Do what works for you.** People have different rhythms. Some people are most productive in the morning; others are only creative in the still of the night. Some people like to work in noisy coffee shops or with music blasting; others need the quiet of a library. Get to know yourself and figure out when and where you do your best learning, writing, and reading.

Good Study Habits

Figuring Out Your Major

Choosing a major is one of the biggest decisions people make in college. In general, students must decide between two academic tracks: preprofessional majors, which are designed to prepare students for specific careers (such as advertising or engineering), and liberal arts majors, which require students to focus on a broader academic subject (such as history or literature). Some schools offer mostly preprofessional majors or mostly liberal arts majors, and others (generally bigger schools) offer both. (Some colleges with less traditional curricula even allow you to design your own major.) There are pros and cons to both types of degree. Proponents of preprofessional programs believe that focusing courses on career goals helps students save time and money. And proponents of liberal arts degrees argue that taking a broad range of courses makes students strong, flexible thinkers and communicators—which in turn makes them desirable to employers in many different fields.

If you already know what you want to do with your future and you're eager to do it immediately after college, a preprofessional major, which would require you to take increasingly specialized courses as you move toward gradua-tion, may be a good option for you. If you are still trying to figure out what you want to do and want to keep your options open, however, becoming a liberal arts major will make it easier for you to explore a variety of areas in greater depth. If you decide to go the liberal arts route, you may need a graduate degree or some other form of post-college education to enter a specific field. But even if you earn a preprofessional degree as an undergraduate, you may also need further education.

Whichever major you choose, it's always a good idea to take courses in a wide range of subjects. College is a time for experi-menting, stretching your mind, and trying on different identities to see which ones really fit. By delving into different subjects that interest you—even in the very back of your mind—you can learn a lot about yourself.

HOW I GOT HERE

I grew up in Woods Hole, Massachusetts, a town that's full of biologists (like my father). We had lots of wild animals when I was a kid—skunks, raccoons, sea gulls—and there was lots of nature going on. Later, as a biology major in college, I got sick of killing mice, so I looked around for labs where you didn't have to kill the studied object and ended up in the psychology department.

PROFESSOR NANCY KANWISHER, COGNITIVE NEUROSCIENTIST (M.I.T.)

Wooster was the perfect match for me because I am very involved in music and it was the only small school that had a large music program. It also is known for its independent studies (an independent study is like a thesis). It sounded very cool to pick a topic and write a huge paper about it before you graduate and relate it to what you are planning to do in the future.

(College of Wooster, OH)

Maybe you've dreamed about being a writer for as long as you can remember. It's possible (in one hypothetical scenario) that your twentieth century English literature classes will be every bit as fascinating as you'd hoped, and that an elective class you take in anthropology will make you a well-rounded writer. But it's also possible (in another hypothetical scenario) that your anthropology class might nudge your career aspirations in a different direction—helping you realize that what you **really** want to do when you grow up is to study human evolution. Discovering your true likes and dislikes and making sure that your academic goals are in line with who you are is an important lesson in and of itself. Whether your academic path ends up fairly straight or takes a few surprising turns, it's always a good idea to take full advantage of the opportunities available to you as a college student.

Its curriculum was very structured and really focused on what I wanted to do, fine arts. (New York University)

PLAGIARISM

A 2003 Rutgers University survey of students from twenty-three colleges found that Internet plagiarism—cutting and pasting other peoples' words from sources located on the Net and claiming them as your own—is on the rise. More disturbingly, perhaps, almost 50 percent of the students surveyed by Rutgers said that they thought an occasional Internet cut-and-paste to enhance a paper was no big deal—or not even cheating at all.

But, really, it is. Whenever students, scholars, or popular writers "borrow" somebody else's words from magazines, books, or online articles without attributing those words to their original source (i.e., using footnotes and quotation marks and citations stating the author, title, and date of the publication), they are claiming certain observations or handsomely turned phrases as their own and, essentially, lying to their readers. This kind of misrepresentation irritates the writers who've been copied and not credited (for obvious reasons), alienates readers (who thought they could trust their favorite mass-market nonfiction writers to be straight with them), and infuriates professors (who don't like being taken for fools by students).

The best way to be honest in your academic work is to make a habit of attributing. And if you're ever unclear about how to distinguish your ideas from someone else's when you're writing a research paper or essay, don't hesitate to ask your professor or a school librarian for help. (If your school has a writing lab, that's a good resource to turn to as well.)

But if you're still not convinced that cheating is a bad idea, you should, at the very least, be aware that it's easier than ever to get caught in the act. Just as a contemporary plagiarizer types a few keywords relating to her subject into an Internet search engine to find a paper to buy or poach, a teacher can later type any suspicious-sounding line from the student's paper into a search engine and find the exact paper the student copied in the first place. Bingo, the student is busted—and, potentially, facing an automatic failing grade in the course or expulsion from the school.

More importantly, though, students who copy other people's work are really cheating themselves. Colleges (and every other kind of school) exist so that people can stretch their minds and become broader, deeper thinkers. And if people don't take that academic challenge seriously—recognizing and appreciating the value of learning for learning's sake—there's no point in spending the time and money that higher education requires.

COLLEGE MAJORS

Some popular majors
Business Administration/Management
Psychology
Elementary Education and Teaching
Biology/Biological Sciences
Nursing
Education
English Language and Literature
Communications Studies/Speech
Communication and Rhetoric
Computer Science
Economics

Some Less Common Majors
African-American Studies
Animal Science
Architectural History
Aviation
Astrophysics
Counseling
Criminal Justice
Equine Studies
Floriculture
Gerontology
Landscape Architecture
Logistics Management
Music Management
Mortuary Science
Oceanography
Sports Management
Urban Planning

The Pre's
Pre-Dentistry
Pre-Law
Pre-Medicine
Pre-Seminary
Pre-Veterinary Medicine

GRADES AND EXPLORATION
Most schools offer students the option to audit classes—to show up, listen, and do as much work as they'd like to do, but without receiving a grade at the end. Many schools also offer students the chance to take a class pass/fail (p/f) or satisfactory/no credit (S/NC). Either of these options provides a great opportunity to take something you're interested in without the pressure of a grade. (If you think you might be interested in graduate school or a job that will look at your college transcript, it's probably not a good idea to take too many pass/fail classes.)

Colorado College has a very interesting, and intense, academic schedule, called the Block Plan. In this plan, you have eight Blocks in a year, each about three to four weeks long. You take a different class each Block. At the end of each Block, you take a final for that class and then move on to the next class. You take only one class at a time. I love it, but it is intense having one class three to four hours a day for a month or so.
(Colorado College, Colorado Springs)

HOW I GOT HERE
While studying classical composition at Oxford, I discovered working in theater, and I did a couple of television things and a student film. I got fed up with the classical route because I wanted to write music and communicate it. After college, I learned my craft over about eight years of working in television.

RACHEL PORTMAN, FILM SCORER

Extracurricular Activities

A common complaint about colleges, which are often separated geographically and demographically from their surrounding communities, is that they bear little resemblance to "real" life. And if you think about it, the criticism is fair: A small city where the vast majority of residents are aged eighteen to twenty-two (which is basically what a college is) would be weird indeed, if such a thing existed in the real world.

Fortunately, though, there are hundreds of extracurricular activities—anything from volunteering at a nearby literacy center to ice skating to setting up a campus campaign organization for your favorite presidential candidate—that can help keep you plugged in to people and ideas outside of the classroom.

The Benefits of Extracurriculars
Add structure to your life and help yourself relax.
Whether you're the type who likes to debate serious topics of the day or scramble up rock walls for kicks, spending a few hours every week pursuing your favorite hobby will help you reduce stress. People like to say that the more you do, the more you can do, and it really is true: Having a mix of activities on your schedule is one of the best ways to develop discipline and efficiency. If you commit to Thursday nights at your school's debate club, say, or join a group that meets every Saturday afternoon at a local climbing wall, and plan ahead to get your homework finished beforehand, you will gain a healthy sense of control over your life. You'll be less inclined to feel that your life is ruled by school (and to resent homework as a result). And when you do come back to your books after an extracurricular, there's a good chance you'll feel refreshed and ready to learn

I think you can look at college as a way to bring some other sort of expertise to your writing. So if you want to do science journalism, get a bio degree, or if you want to do design journalism, get an architecture degree. I had these very romantic ideas of covering wars and figured that International Relations was a great degree to have, so that's what I got. It's funny because my career has taken a decidedly domestic slant.
TAMALA EDWARDS,
JOURNALIST

HOW I GOT HERE

I'm in a few of the bands and some other groups, such as the Skydiving Club. We have fun and you make a lot of friends.
(Ohio State University, Columbus)

Gain practical experience you can use in the real world. Participating in a community service project or a campus organization, such as your school newspaper, will teach you valuable life lessons about communication and collaboration, and possibly even lead you to a career you'd like to pursue after college. No matter what you choose to do, your extracurricular activities will help distinguish your talents and interests to potential employers down the line.

Find a cause and connect with like-minded people. Is there an issue that you feel passionate about? Maybe it's the substandard living conditions of poor people near your school, or a proposal to pave over your favorite soccer field. But rather than sit and stew, why not do something about it? You may be able to join an existing campus or community organization fighting for the cause you believe in, or you may have to recruit some of your fellow students and people from the neighborhood near your school to start an organization yourself. But either way, the experience of expressing your ideas and working together with others to make the world a better place will be empowering. And fun, too: When people are mutually committed to the same goal, they often form lasting friendships.

Participating in a community service project or a campus organization, such as your school newspaper, will teach you valuable life lessons about communication and collaboration, and possibly even lead you to a career you'd like to pursue after college. No matter what you choose to do, your extracurricular activities will help distinguish your talents and interests to potential employers down the line.

Get involved in the extracurriculars. That's where you get a break from your program and meet different people. If you're a math major, it's great to hang out with the art or psychology people because, on the whole, they approach life in a different way. Plus extracurriculars are a blast. I joined Habitat for Humanity and it was so good to get outside and work after weeks in the classroom.
(Concordia University, Seward, NE)

I do drama and newspaper. It is very fun to have nonacademic things to do at school.
(Vassar College, Poughkeepsie, NY))

Extracurriciular activities can also be a chance to get a grant or additional financial aid once you are a student. For example, if you work in student government, there is usually grant money for active students. Also, sports teams can provide you with additional funding for your studies. Be sure to research any and all opportunities.

My favorite experiences have been non-academic. Hmm . . .
(Harvard University, Cambridge, MA)

I'm involved in a feminist group. We have fun. We do things for a cause, and we also goof off. I've never been in a group like this before. It's been fun. On a weekend we might get together with others and drink, or go bowling, or watch a movie.
(University of Las Vegas, NV)

SPORTS

Since the Title IX civil rights act was passed into law in 1972, and colleges' eligibility for federal funding hinged upon their providing equal athletic programming for women and men, the number of women in school sports has increased almost 800 percent. Women's college athletics still haven't earned the same level of national attention as men's, but more and more female college athletes are going on to become professional sports superstars. (After playing on the University of North Carolina women's soccer team as it won four consecutive NCAA championship titles, Mia Hamm went on to lead the US women's national team to victory in the 1999 World Cup.)

Most colleges offer students a variety of ways to participate in sports—on varsity teams, as club members, or in less formal intramural leagues. So no matter who you are and what your athletic background has been, it'll be easy to find a rewarding way to compete in the sport (or sports) you love during college.

If you played a sport seriously in high school and you haven't been recruited by a college coach, you may still be able to make your college's varsity team. (Call or drop by the varsity coach's office to learn more about the team you're interested in and if and when it's offering tryouts, but bear in mind that the higher the school's National College Athletic Association rank, the tougher it will be to make the cut.) But even if you're not quite varsity material—or are a total newcomer to organized sports—you can still play in other ways. Your college's athletic department should be able to steer you toward the practice times and contact persons for any club or intramural sport you're interested in. And if you keep your eyes peeled for pickup games in local parks or fliers on bulletin boards—or assemble some like-minded jocks on your own—you can also participate in regular informal team games of basketball, soccer, and Ultimate Frisbee.

The time commitment involved with any college sport is definitely something to consider. If you're an NCAA Division I athlete, you will be

Although I had good grades in hard courses as a freshman biochemistry major, I began to doubt my interest in the field and questioned whether I had even chosen the right college. I became anxious, depressed and paranoid . . . I consulted a psychologist at the campus health center.

After tests and talk revealed no underlying mental illness, the therapist suggested that I find an activity that I might enjoy and that would help me feel more a part of college life. So I joined my college's monthly magazine, began writing and editing science-related articles and eventually realized that my passion lay in writing about science rather than doing it. The rest is history.

JANE E. BRODY,
HEALTH COLUMNIST,
THE NEW YORK TIMES

HOW I GOT HERE

Being with the team kind of is my social life. We
had an initial bond from the start—we knew
right away that we had something in common—
and the team has become like a family to me.
(University of Wisconsin, Madison)

Michigan State students are a friendly, diverse group
with a wealth of opportunities to take advantage of, on
and off campus. There is a thriving student-run newspaper,
a literary journal and several of the nation's most competitive
collegiate and intramural athletic teams.
(Michigan State University, East Lansing)

required to practice with your team about twenty hours a week, and
possibly, encouraged to do even more workouts on your own. If you're a
relatively casual participant in a club sport, you might still be expected
to practice five or more hours a week. Still, the consensus among student
athletes (and former student athletes) is that college sports help people
learn to balance study, sleep, and social time wisely. In addition to building
discipline, college sports help people connect closely with others who
share the same interests, and women who play sports in college enjoy
the camaraderie of teammates.

Even if you aren't into competitive sports, it's important to make
physical activity a regular part of your college life. The stress-reducing
benefits of exercise are dramatic: Regular aerobic activity lowers adren-
aline (the harmful stress hormone that prepares the body to fight or
take flight), decreases a woman's risk of heart attack and stroke (even
thirty minutes of brisk walking a day), and lowers the risk of depression.
Plus, our worries seem smaller when we get away from them for a while.
As the nineteenth-century philosopher Soren Kierkegaard put it: "Above
all, do not lose the desire to walk; every day I walk myself into a state of
well-being and walk away from every illness. I have walked myself into
my best thoughts and I know of no thought so burdensome that one
cannot walk away from it. The more one sits still, the closer one comes
to feeling ill."

Experts are still debating the amount of exercise necessary for optimal
physical and mental health. But for now, the American College of Sports
Medicine and the Centers for Disease Control and Prevention recommend
that men and women walk briskly for at least thirty minutes most days
of the week, or get an equivalent amount of exercise another way, such as
running, rollerblading, or biking. In addition to aerobic activity, both
groups also recommend strength training two to three days a week to
stimulate bone and muscle growth. (Though there's mostly anecdotal
evidence of this so far, psychologists have also noted that weight training
seems to boost women's moods—the theory being that physical strength
increases feelings of emotional strength.)

Finally, participating in any kind of regular athletic activity—whether it's part of a formal team sport program or your own independent gym regimen—can really help you eat healthily and feel your best in college. On top of fighting stress and burning calories, frequent exercise tends to make people crave low-fat, high-protein fueling foods rather than empty, sugary calories (such as ice cream). So if you're an athlete, your body will automatically remind you that it's better to fill up on whole grains, fruits, and vegetables instead of chips.

FOR INFO ON EATING WELL ON CAMPUS, SEE P. 92.

Campus Life

SOCIAL LIFE

Every college has a different social scene, determined by many factors, including the school's size and location, whether or not it has fraternities and sororities, and, most important, the kind of students it attracts. At small colleges in rural areas, social life tends to revolve around sporting events and campus parties (Greek, dorm, house parties, or otherwise). At large urban universities, the social scene is usually more varied, with some students staying on campus for dorm and frat parties, and others heading out to clubs and concerts around town.

To make your free time as rewarding as possible over the next four years, it's important to keep your own social style and interests in mind as you choose a school. Are you the kind of person who likes to unwind on Saturday night by playing a mellow game of cards with a few friends? If so, you might want to avoid a college famous for its head-bangingly loud beer bashes. Are you a culture vulture who needs movies and museums to feel alive? Then you might want to consider a big city university—or a smaller college that gets great movies on campus and sponsors regular field trips to regional museums. Since extracurricular activities will help you

FOR MORE ON FRATERNITIES AND SORORITIES, SEE P. 89.

make friends and explore possible career paths, make sure to look for a school that offers organizations and clubs in line with your interests.

You probably won't find a college that's a 100-percent perfect reflection of your personality—hardly anyone does. But it is important to make sure that the pluses of any given college outweigh the minuses for you. The best way to get a sense of the student body and its diversity or lack thereof is (once again) to visit the campus. Talking to students about their typical activities will help you decide if a school is right for you.

And bear in mind, if you find a school that seems perfect for you in lots of ways but the social things you're looking for don't seem readily available, they are very likely hidden somewhere, if the school is big enough. Colleges are microcosms of the world—if you go to a beer-blast college, you can still find quiet corners and people whose intellectual interests overlap with your own.

HOUSING

Every school has different housing arrangements. Depending on a school's location and size, students might live in dorms or college-owned apartments, in privately owned off-campus apartments, at home with their families, or in a variety of different types of housing. Where you live will have a big impact on your college experience—in a lot of ways, your roommates and neighbors become a support system—so weigh your options carefully.

Although the campus spans several acres and can seem overwhelming at times, the great variety of living options makes the school feel more personal and does a good job of meeting most residents' social and academic needs. Many students choose dorms based on the academic interests represented there: everything from arts and letters to medicine and law.
(Michigan State University, East Lansing)

Living on Campus

To ease the transition from living at home and help students get to know their classmates, many colleges require or recommend that first-year students live in campus dorms and sign up for college meal plans that require them to eat one or more meals a day in campus cafeterias. Dorm living provides an immersive environment for new college students. Many freshmen travel in packs first semester as they enjoy their first heady months away from home. These geographically motivated friendships may last a lifetime—or may fizzle before Christmas break to make way for new social circles.

The intimate housing system produces close friendships and, frequently, intense drama. Unlike large and impersonal dorms, the houses foster a complete community.
(Smith College, Northampton, MA)

Most freshman dorms have resident advisers—sophomores or upper-classmen trained in counseling and crisis management. RAs are on hand to help supervise students and give them assistance with any personal or academic problems that may arise.

Freshmen living on campus are usually assigned a roommate or roommates of the same sex in a coed or single-sex hall (though many schools are building more single rooms). Some schools use detailed computer surveys to pair up students according to their musical tastes, sleep and study routines, and housekeeping habits. Other schools more or less randomly assign students to room together.

Regardless of how sophisticated the roommate matchmaking process has been, living and sleeping in a small space with a relative stranger can be challenging at first. You and your roommate may or may not become best friends. But if you and she can communicate your needs to each other openly and respectfully—and realize that you're both going to have to compromise from time to time—there's a good chance you'll get along and enjoy each other's company.

Living Off-Campus

Upperclassmen who want to cook and otherwise fend for themselves often decide to move off campus after living in dorms for a year or two. But occasionally first-year students at big schools with housing shortages are required to find their own housing, too. (Note: If this happens to you, you may want to consider signing up for a campus meal plan anyway. Dining on campus can help you meet your classmates and save time if you aren't ready to assume the responsibility of shopping and cooking for yourself.)

College students usually say that independence and privacy are the advantages of living off campus. But it can be cheaper, too—in some areas, renting a studio apartment for one or sharing a bigger apartment with others costs significantly less than living in school-owned housing. Your campus housing office should be able to provide listings for off-campus apartments or recommend landlords that students have successfully rented from in the past. Local newspapers, bulletin boards in grocery stores and laundromats, and roommate-locating services are also good places to find apartment listings.

COMMUTER SCHOOLS

Though some of the following urban schools do provide housing for freshmen students, many or most of the students at these schools (just a sampling) live off campus and commute to class:

Boston University (Boston, MA)
Cooper Union for the Advancement of Science and Art (New York, NY)
Creighton University (Omaha, NE)
John Jay College of Criminal Justice (New York, NY)
Northeastern University (Boston, MA)
University of California (Los Angeles)
University of Illinois (Chicago)
University of Texas (Arlington)
University of Wisconsin (Milwaukee)

DORM DECORATING

If you've visited schools or flipped through college view-books, you already know that, for the most part, college dormitories aren't what you'd call elegant—especially on the inside. Cinderblock walls and simple, solidly built furniture are the common denominators of most dorm rooms. But with ingenuity and a few favorite posters or pillows, it is possible to transform a dorm room into a cheerful, personalized, homey space.

ROOMMATES

Sharing a room with someone can be weird, especially if you've always had your own space. Chances are, both of you will be pretty nervous about how you'll get along. Even if you and your roommate hit it off, it's not particularly likely that you will end up being best friends. Hanging out with someone all the time and living in the same room with them inevitably leads to some tension-filled moments.

As in any relationship, keep the lines of communication open so you can deal with problems as they come up. Try to set some ground rules, particularly about cleaning and study or sleep schedules. It will probably take a while to get to know each other's personal habits, but it's not a bad idea to talk about how you would handle some common potentially awkward roomie scenarios, such as how to avoid being "sexiled" (being locked out of your room while your roommate hooks up with someone). But most roommates at least have mutual respect for one another.

If it looks like things aren't working out, there are resources available to you. RAs are trained to deal with roommate situations. Many schools will allow you to change rooms (and sometimes roommates), but it depends on their policy; some are strict and allow changes only in dire situations, while others are relatively easygoing.

Sometimes you and your roommate might seem totally incompatible. But you may end up meeting someone you never would have met otherwise, and they might introduce you to new ideas and people. On the other hand, maybe they'll be someone you would never want to meet otherwise. Either way, adjusting to a roommate is a big part of the freshman learning experience.

Living in Affiliated Housing

Many campuses provide campus housing for people who are affiliated with a certain group—international students, pre-med students, or other social communities—on the understanding that it can be a comfort to be surrounded by people who speak the same language, have similar interests, or are facing some of the same challenges. At some schools, you can gain access to this type of housing simply by requesting it, while in other places you may need to apply.

Living at Home

For various reasons, including comfort and cost, students sometimes choose to continue living at home with their parents during college. Because college is typically a time when people take more control of their lives, it would be a good idea to talk to your parents and siblings about your expectations and theirs if you're planning on living at home while you earn your degree. Depending on the length of your commute, your course schedule, and your social life, you may end up seeing your parents less than you did in high school. If you let your parents know what you're up to and contribute to the household upkeep, chances are they'll treat you like the adult you are becoming. Try to establish the terms of your living at home (if and when you are expected home, what happens if you don't come home, etc.).

Living in a Sorority or Fraternity

Often, college fraternities and sororities have their own houses, where member students live and socialize together. These houses can be crowded, and as a result, there's not much privacy. But depending on the house, the cost of living in a fraternity or sorority, which usually also includes meals, can be cheaper than on-campus room and board. Since regular meetings and parties take place in most houses, they tend to attract social people, and for people who are comfortable being around a lot of people a lot of the time (not to mention lots of partying), they can be pleasant places to live.

FOR MORE INFORMATION ON FRATERNITIES AND SORORITIES, SEE P. 89.

COLLEGIATE HOUSING AND ALCOHOL CONSUMPTION
According to studies conducted by the National Institute of Alcohol and Alcoholism, student drinking varies in different kinds of housing. Drinking rates are highest in fraternities and sororities, followed by on-campus housing. Students who live in independent housing (such as off-campus apartments) drink less, and students who live at home with their families and commute to campus drink the least.

ALSO SEE P. 95 FOR MORE INFORMATION ON DRINKING AND DRUGS.

SAFETY

Colleges—in urban areas and elsewhere—are not immune to crimes. The prevalence of students walking alone at night and of expensive computers and stereos in dorm rooms make college campuses and their surrounding areas attractive to criminals. Disturbingly, the majority of petty and violent crimes (including sexual assaults) on college campuses—an estimated 80 percent—are committed by students themselves. In a number of studies, student alcohol consumption has been linked to these increases in campus crime.

According to the US Department of Education, the number of murders committed on college campuses declined by 1999, but the number of sexual offenses, robberies, and hate crimes all increased. In response to growing public awareness of campus robberies and assaults, laws have been passed that require colleges to provide students and potential students with basic campus crime statistics and to disclose information about registered sex offenders who are either enrolled at or employed by the school. (You should be able to find out about campus crime statistics and security policies from the admissions office or office of student life at any school you're considering.) Many colleges across the country have also tightened campus security in recent years, hiring more campus police and establishing closer working relationships with local police departments, which can assist with the investigation and prosecution of campus crime.

At any college you're looking at, it's important to feel that the administration is both acknowledging campus crime (as opposed to sweeping it under the rug) and taking serious steps to stop it. Campus building entrances and walkways should always be brightly lit at night, and there should be many prominently displayed security phones (preferably illuminated with a distinctively colored light) around a campus and its outskirts. A school should provide a free shuttle service or a student safety escort twenty-four hours a day to any place students might need to travel on or near campus. Some schools provide dormitory guards who require students and their guests to show photo identification, day and night. But at the very least, dorm buildings should be fitted with strong locks and students required to keep them locked at all times.

There are also important steps you can take to protect yourself in college. Always lock your dorm room door when you're sleeping. If you are going to be studying late at the library or attending a party after dark, set a time and place where you'll meet friends or fellow residents of your dorm to walk home. Or catch a ride on the campus shuttle. It might be a pain to take the shuttle at 2:00 a.m. when you could just walk, but it is much better to be safe than sorry.

College crime is most likely here to stay. But you can dramatically reduce your personal risk by being aware of dangerous situations and taking steps to avoid them.

FOR MORE ON DATE RAPE, SEE P. 103.

Fraternities and Sororities

At large universities and small colleges, you're likely to find sororities (literally, societies of "sisters") and fraternities (societies of "brothers"—though some fraternities are coed). Typically, sororities and fraternities have their own houses, designated with three letters of the Greek alphabet, where member students live and socialize. According to the National Interfraternity Conference, only about 12 percent of college students are members of fraternities and sororities. But depending on the school, the Greek system can either play a small part in student life or take center stage on the social scene.

To join a fraternity or sorority, students must participate in a formal recruitment process known as "rush." Rush procedures differ from school to school. Typically, however, freshmen or sophomores interested in the Greek system attend meet-and-greet "rush week" parties hosted by various fraternities and sororities on campus to see how they get along with the members. If a student decides not to pursue membership herself, she's free to drop out of rush at any point. But if a student decides she would like to join a specific Greek group, the feeling must be mutual—that is, the sorority or fraternity must also formally invite her to join by becoming a "pledge."

For obvious reasons, students who aren't chosen by their favorite fraternities and sororities are sometimes left with bad feelings about rush. Fraternity and sorority members who make the cut, however, enjoy the feeling of instant belonging—making "automatic friends for life," as one student puts it. To many, the appeal of the Greek system is that it offers students a home base on campus and a group of students who share a unifying goal—which, in the case of sororities, is often described as a commitment to female scholarship, physical fitness, and school leadership. Since active alumni members of fraternities and sororities help students network to land jobs after graduation, there's also a strong sense in the Greek system that the perks of membership will extend well beyond college.

I am in a sorority, so we do a lot of community service and plan things for school. I really love it. I sometimes do things with my sorority and some-times just with some of the girls from there. We go out and go dancing or go to a party or just sometimes have a quiet coffee at a coffee house. (University of California, Los Angeles)

AFFILIATED SORORITIES
Some sororities draw their membership from women of a particular religion or ethnicity (this is not a formal arrangement, and it varies from school to school). Some examples:
Asian: Chi Alpha Delta, Sigma Phi Omega
Black: Alpha Kappa Alpha, Zeta Phi Beta
Christian: Alpha Delta Chi, Phi Beta Chi
Jewish: Alpha Epsilon Phi, Sigma Delta Tau
Latina: Sigma Lambda Alpha, Kappa Delta Chi
Multicultural: Theta Nu Xi, Sigma Omega Phi

Still, fraternities and sororities have some major public relations problems. Though some politically sensitized fraternities and sororities have begun actively recruiting more diverse students, exclusivity is still a big part of the Greek system, where membership is often determined by factors like personal appearance, family background, and social class. At various times, reports of extreme physical and emotional abuse of pledges, as part of "hazing" indoctrination rituals, have shocked the nation.

And then there's the issue of alcohol. The popular image of Greek parties as beer-soaked bacchanalias is something that many fraternity and sorority members feel compelled to uphold, but the consequences of pushing the limits can be dire. Several pledges have died in the last few years due to drinking excessively at fraternity parties or initiation ceremonies, and many more have been seriously injured.

To combat negative publicity and keep students safe, many universities and colleges, such as MIT, Wisconsin, and Dartmouth, have drastically cracked down on underage drinking in fraternities and sororities in recent years. Several colleges, including Bowdoin, Williams, Middlebury, and Colby, have even shut down Greek houses on campus entirely. Some fraternities and sororities have also tried to clean up their own images by requiring members to become active volunteers. According to the National Interfraternity Conference, members now perform ten million hours of service annually. Yet different data—such as the National Institute on Alcohol Abuse's 2002 finding that colleges where Greek systems dominate have the highest binge drinking rate—suggest that alcohol is still a major part of Greek life.

As with most things in life, there are pros and cons to fraternities and sororities. Only you can decide if the Greek system suits your personality and social style. But if you are thinking you'd like to participate in a Greek group, make certain that you enjoy the other house members, feel okay about the time commitment required (which can be considerable, especially for new pledges), and, most importantly, respect the group's philosophy and practices.

Being a member of a group you respect and that respects you can be a powerful and positive thing. But feeling like membership in the group requires you to change some part of yourself to fit in, or to turn a blind eye to activities that you know are wrong, is not fun at all. In college—and beyond—it's always important to make sure that any group you're considering joining really "gets" who you are and will allow you to be who you really are.

Taking Charge of Your Health

Living on your own for the first time is an exciting, challenging experience and also, sometimes, a stressful one. When your environment and your schedule totally changes, health concerns can often become a low priority. But it's as important as ever to take care of your health—especially since you are now in charge of it.

You probably already know what you need to do to safeguard your health over the long and short term: exercise regularly; eat a well-balanced, nutritional diet; and get the sleep you need. But the older you get, the more you will appreciate the benefits of being healthy. Taking good care of yourself in college will help you boost your immune system to fight off common illnesses such as colds and flus, which are easily passed from student to student on a busy college campus. And it will help you protect your mental health, giving you the energy and resources you need to handle stress without becoming overly anxious or depressed.

STRESS

Lots of students feel like they're trying to cram too much into too little time: jobs, schoolwork, relationships, and extracurriculars, to name a few. Stress is a natural response to changes in your environment, but sometimes it can get out of control. Experts say that to ward off stress, you should exercise (to relieve tension), eat well (to keep you energized), and get enough sleep (so you can stay focused). Stay away from caffeine and sugar in particular: they tend to send the body into cycles of hyperactivity and crashing.

If you're feeling stressed, the first thing you can do is work on managing your time. Prioritize your schedule and make sure there's room in every day for what you need to do. If your coursework is overwhelming, consider dropping a class or changing your status in it to audit or pass/fail (if those are options at your school).

Then, try to schedule time to play: find something you like to do and do it every day. You could make time for yourself by writing in a journal, sketching, going for a walk, or listening to music. You can also target stress directly through relaxation techniques like yoga and meditation.

Some ways of coping with stress, like smoking, drinking, or even eating comfort foods, may seem like solutions but end up making things worse. Recent studies have shown that smoking causes rather than eliminates stress. Drinking to relax is a short-term solution, and can be addictive if it becomes a habit. And compulsive eating might start out as a reaction to stress but escalate into an eating disorder.

If you feel like your stress levels are skyrocketing, talk to someone. Sit down with a friend or professor and sort out how you're feeling. Or, call a counselor through student health services. Most schools have resources—especially during exam time—to help people who are feeling overwhelmed. Don't be shy about seeking help.

College is a great time to take charge of your health and learn a lot more about how your own body works. Access to campus health services is usually included in the price of tuition (or available to students for a nominal price), and you should freely take advantage of this great service. It's important—always—to visit a doctor at the first sign that an illness might be serious (serious symptoms include high fever or severe pain) and to get into the habit of taking yourself in for annual checkups. Campus doctors and nurses are specially trained to talk to people your age, and they know a lot about the physical problems that young people face (or just worry about). So even when you're healthy, visiting campus health services—and asking plenty of questions—can give you tremendous peace of mind.

YOUR MENTAL HEALTH

Some colleges offer mental health services in their health departments, and others offer counseling through their departments of student life. But it's a safe bet that your school provides some form of confidential mental health service, somewhere. And if you're ever feeling emotionally overwhelmed—by homesickness, your course load, relationships, or any other imaginable life concern—do not be afraid to seek help for mental health problems. For some people in some situations, it's hard to talk about problems with their families and friends, and that's when therapy or counseling can really be beneficial. Campus mental health experts are there to help you understand your problems and to work toward solutions that feel right to you. They can help you understand more clearly situations that seem strange and scary, and they can teach you how to communicate your feelings to the people who are important in your life. They can put you in touch with support groups on campus where you can meet and talk to students who are in similar situations, and they can make sure you receive proper medication, if that's something you need. Talking about your private concerns with people you don't know well can feel awkward at first, but the process has helped many people to overcome difficult patches in their lives—and to come out stronger on the other side.

EATING WELL ON CAMPUS

Eating well is an important part of your overall health. But college freshmen are notorious for eating poorly. With all-you-can-eat buffets and ice cream bars at every meal, it's no wonder.

Eating a balanced diet is actually one of the best things you can do for your body. As the old standby USDA Food Pyramid suggests, eat lots of fruit and vegetables and minimal fats. In the dining hall, check out what they're serving before you decide what you want. Beware of empty calories, like soda and frozen soft-serve desserts. Even if you're getting takeout, some options are healthier and more nutritious than others. Go for pizza with veggies on top instead of extra cheese; opt for roasted chicken instead of deep-fried. With the late-night hours typical of many students—whether you're up studying or partying—come the dangers of late-night snacking. Plan for this by stocking healthy snacks (yogurt or fruit, for instance) in your minifridge.

EATING DISORDERS

It's difficult to estimate how many people suffer from eating disorders because not everyone seeks help, but it is thought that 5 to 20 percent of college women suffer from some sort of disordered eating. Because eating disorders are so common, most colleges offer counselors, discussion groups, or other resources through student health services.

While there are several distinct types of eating disorders, many sufferers share similar traits: Most have a distorted perception of how they look, and as they lose weight, they still think they're too fat. They also may have extreme weight fluctuations and an obsession with eating and their weight.

ANOREXIA NERVOSA may start as a diet and turn into an unhealthy obsession. People who suffer from anorexia nervosa are often high achievers who like to control the world around them. Anorexics eat barely enough to survive and often lose weight rapidly. They may even avoid situations where they have to eat, or have specific rules about what, when, and how to eat.

BULIMIA involves bingeing and purging. Bulimics eat more food than they think they should eat. Then they get it out of their system by throwing up or taking laxatives and diuretics. Many bulimics can hide their problems by bingeing and purging in secret, though this is harder to do in a public bathroom or dorm. Long-term bulimia wreaks havoc on the body, destroying tooth enamel and harming internal organs.

BINGE EATING DISORDER is the most common—and the most recently recognized—eating disorder. Binge eaters eat huge amounts of food at a time, eating until they are uncomfortably full. But they don't purge afterward; instead, they may feel disgusted, guilty, and depressed. Many binge eaters are obese and binge as a result of deprivation diets. They may avoid social situations and, like other sufferers of eating disorders, keep their problem a secret.

In addition to these common, diagnosable eating disorders, many people, college girls in particular, obsess about eating, exercise, and weight, and this can be dangerous too. Unhealthy behaviors range from occasionally bingeing and/or purging, to not eating enough to maintain your period (menstruating requires a minimum threshold of body fat), to exercising for three hours a day. While they may not have a full-fledged eating disorder, they might be on their way to one—and they probably aren't treating their bodies very well in the meantime.

If you think you may have an eating disorder (or if you know somebody who does), talk to somebody at Student Health Services.

There's also the spectre of the dreaded "Freshman 15." Research shows that freshmen gain an average of a few pounds in the first twelve weeks of school. It's not inevitable though. Weight gain can be avoided if you eat a balanced diet, learn what a portion is and serve yourself accordingly, and avoid unconscious eating. Another good idea: Eat breakfast! Studies show that people who skip meals tend to eat more calories during the day than those who eat a balanced breakfast in the morning. Plus, you'll perform better in those morning classes.

EXERCISE

Regular exercise is always a good idea: It keeps you fit, reduces stress, and minimizes health problems, such as depression and insomnia. And college campuses make it easier than ever to fit exercise into your schedule. On a large enough campus, simply walking from class to class is a good aerobic workout.

Varsity and intramural sports as well as sports clubs provide plenty of structure and variety for people who enjoy organized sports—whether it's something rigorous, like crew, or something laid back, like Ultimate Frisbee (a GREAT workout!). And most colleges have terrific facilities—swimming pools, tracks, and gyms—that are available to anyone with a student ID. If you like company while you work out, find someone to join you!

FOR MORE ON COLLEGE SPORTS, SEE P. 80.

DRINKING AND DRUGS

College is a time when many people are drinking and doing drugs for the first time—or drinking and doing drugs more than ever before, now that they're on their own. For this reason it's a good idea to re-evaluate your own attitudes and concerns about drugs as you move into this next phase of your life. In order to make responsible decisions about drugs and alcohol for yourself, it's important to have a sense of WHY you might want to use and WHAT the effects and risks (not to mention legal status) of a particular drug might be.

Drugs on Campus

Though the use of marijuana has been common on college campuses since the sixties, the popularity of hard drugs, such as coke, speed, and LSD, has fluctuated. Oftentimes, a certain drug becomes fashionable, associated with a certain kind of collegiate party scene. Recently, the illegal use of prescription drugs, such as Xanax, a sedative, and Ritalin, a form of amphetamine that many people take for Attention Deficit Disorder, has become more common on campuses as students "self-medicate."

Since the use of medications for mood and attention disorders has become widespread in almost every age group, it's easier for students to get medications like these from friends or family members who take them legitimately. Heavily trafficked Internet drugstores—which send drugs (often of uncertain quality and chemical composition) to anyone with a computer and a credit card—also make it simple for students to procure drugs online (although a federal task force is attempting to put an end to these illegal sales). To avoid the potentially catastrophic consequences of self-medicating, it is extremely important for students (or anyone else) experiencing depression, anxiety, or difficulty concentrating to consult a health-care professional, who will have an arsenal of treatment options.

SMOKY THINKING?
More than 28 percent of college students smoke, and many of them started in college.
Why? Peer pressure? The desire to seem mature and sophisticated? Who knows?
One thing is clear. Smoking has been proven to dramatically increase the risk of virtually every major disease. Think carefully about what makes sense for you and your health!

FOR RESOURCES ON DRINKING AND DRUGS, SEE P. 107.

FOUR-YEAR COLLEGES

ALCOHOL

On almost every college campus, alcohol is by far the number-one drug of choice. Drinking is often seen as an integral part of college life. Some people consider college drinking as a harmless rite of passage, a simple part of fitting into the social scene. Others, however, see it as a serious public health problem.

FOR MORE ON ALCOHOL USE IN FRATERNITIES AND SORORITIES, SEE P. 89.

Alcohol is a depressant that sedates the central nervous system. Since drinking tends to produce feelings of well-being and confidence at first, many college students use alcohol as a "social lubricant" to help them relax and forget their problems. Initially, alcohol affects thought, emotion, and judgment, but after a while, it impairs speech, muscle coordination, and makes people sleepy. Consumed in massive quantities, alcohol can even result in coma and death.

College drinking can be low-key: a few students getting together to drink a six-pack of beer in somebody's dorm room. Or it can be pretty intense: As part of certain fraternities' initiation rites, pledges are occasionally forced to chug grain alcohol until they pass out.

Recognizing the risks of college drinking, many colleges have cracked down on drinking on campus in the last decade or so. But no matter how stringent your school's alcohol policies, you're probably going to encounter situations where people are drinking soon after you arrive at school. Whether or not to join them is up to you, but it is very important to understand the risks of college drinking (beyond simply being illegal until you're twenty-one) as you make your own decisions.

Binge Drinking

Though plenty of college students choose to drink moderately or not at all, many—44 percent, according to the National Institute of Alcohol and Alcoholism—drink to excess on a regular basis. Among college students, binge drinking, which the NIAA defines as five consecutive drinks for men and four drinks for women, has been linked to drinking and driving, poor academic performance, and medical and legal problems. Overdose is extremely common among binge drinkers. According to the NIAA and the Centers for Disease Control:

> **Underage alcohol use is more likely to kill young people than all illegal drugs combined.**

> **Alcohol consumption is linked to at least 1,400 student deaths and 500,000 injuries annually.**

Alcohol use interacts with conditions such as depression and stress to contribute to suicide, the third leading cause of death among people between the ages of fourteen and twenty-five.

The Hazards of Alcohol for Women

For years, drinking a small amount (one glass of wine or beer a day) was thought to have health benefits for women. But new scientific data suggests otherwise: The risk of breast cancer appears to increase by 30 percent with as little as one drink per day, and the risk increases significantly with each drink beyond that. Because women are generally smaller than men and produce less alcohol dehydrogenase, the enzyme that metabolizes alcohol, women get drunk faster than men. Overall, women drink less than men, but women who drink heavily over the long term are more likely than men to suffer from alcohol's adverse effects, including damage to the liver and heart.

There are also short-term consequences of drinking that particularly affect women. Since alcohol impairs judgment, women who drink heavily are more likely to engage in high-risk, unprotected sex—which sometimes results in unwanted pregnancy and sexually transmitted disease. Women who drink heavily in college are also particularly vulnerable to sexual assault. So from every angle, it's clear that moderation is key for women who do want to drink.

What's Too Far?

With drugs, alcohol and peer pressure as omnipresent as they are on campuses, it's extremely important to think about how you plan to approach drinking and drugs in college. It's really up to you to make sure that drinking or drugs—whether it be your own or other people's—does not adversely affect your life. Try to develop coping strategies for tough times (talking with understanding friends or a campus counselor, or even exercising) so that if you feel yourself becoming overwhelmed by stress or unfamiliar new emotions (something that happens to every college student), you'll be less likely to turn to alcohol or drugs to make yourself feel better.

People act unpredictably when they're under the influence of alcohol or any other drug. But if you set your own limits and boundaries, rather than just accepting someone else's idea of a good time—you will greatly reduce the risk of alcohol interfering with your happiness and safety in college and beyond.

Drugs and alcohol can be addictive. If you think that you or a friend might have a problem, it's important to seek help.

FOR RESOURCES ON DEALING WITH ALCOHOL AND ADDICTION, SEE P. 107.

SEX

As you move into your college years, gaining independence (most likely living on your own for the first time, with no one to monitor your behavior) and forming new relationships, you may need to make some new choices about sex for yourself.

As a consenting adult, you're free to approach sex however you like, to have it or not have it with whoever you like. Whether you decide to have sex, to abstain, or to wait and see how a relationship unfolds is entirely up to you. The important thing is to feel comfortable in any sexual situation—be it intercourse, giving or receiving oral sex, or just a kiss.

Are You Ready to Do It?

For many people in college, one of the biggest questions about sex is whether or not to have it—for the very first time, or with somebody new. According to different surveys, 46 percent of high school seniors in the United States have had sexual intercourse, and 71 percent of college students describe themselves as having had sexual experience—so it's pretty clear that more people are becoming sexually active in college.

If you're a virgin and you enter into a relationship in college, the subject of sex is likely to come up before too long. But it's important not to rush into things. There are some very important questions that virgins and non-virgins alike should ask themselves before deciding whether or not to have sex with someone new. Most importantly, you should be clear that you trust and care for the person, and feel comfortable enough to talk openly about your past sexual histories. It's essential that you both assume responsibility for having sex safely. If you are at all unsure when you think about any aspect of having sex with this person, pay serious attention to that feeling!

At any stage of life, saying no to someone who wants sex when you don't can be difficult. But no matter how uncomfortable you feel saying no, you'll feel better than you would if you'd had sex against your better judgment.

Reproductive Health

If you've decided you're ready to have sex, or you're having sex already, it's essential that you do it safely. To protect yourself and your partner from sexually transmitted diseases (STDs) and protect yourself from getting pregnant, make sure you educate yourself on various birth control methods (if you're having sex with a man) and methods for preventing the spread of STDs (whether you're having sex with a man or a woman). Making a commitment to protecting your sexual health and your partner's is part of being a responsible human being.

Unfortunately, college students do not talk about safe-sex protection before sex, or use protection during sex, nearly as often as they should. According to one recent survey of college students, only 56 percent of males and 55 percent of females reported discussing birth control with their partner before their last sexual encounter, and only 46 percent of males and 48 percent of females reported using a condom during their most recent sexual encounter. More encouragingly, however, the same survey detected that talking about sex and the relationship beforehand really does help people do it more safely.

EXPERIMENTATION

College is often a place for experimentation—and sometimes a place where sexuality is called into question. The freedom of being away from home inspires many students to "try out" things they might otherwise have repressed. While these interactions can sometimes be a step in the direction of a particular lifestyle, just as often, they are part of establishing a sexual independence and trying things on for size.

For those who are still in the process of exploring their sexual preferences—as well as those who aren't sure what they're into, but so far lack any actual physical experience—college can be a confusing time. But it can also be exciting and extremely fulfilling. Fortunately, as in other collegiate arenas, there's a good chance that there will be like-minded people around who are experiencing similar feelings of confusion, excitement, and self-discovery.

BIRTH CONTROL BASICS

Abstinence is the only 100 percent effective form of birth control and it's your best protections against STDs too.

TYPE OF BIRTH CONTROL	EFFECTIVENESS AGAINST PREGNANCY
ABSTINENCE	**100%**
HORMONAL METHODS, which a woman takes through patches, shots, pills, or implants.	birth control pills, shots (Depo-Provera), implants (Norplant), all **99%**
BARRIER METHODS, such as male and female condoms, diaphragms, and cervical caps. Only condoms prevent STDs.	male condoms, **88%** female condoms, **90%** diaphragms (with spermicide), **82%** cervical cap (with spermicide), **82%**
SPERMICIDES, which come in jellies, creams, foams, and suppositories, are most effective in stopping pregnancy when used in conjunction with barrier methods.	when used alone, **79%**
An **IUD**, or intrauterine device, which is inserted into the uterus by a health professional. Shaped like a T, these small inserts release either copper or progesterone ions, which prevent fertilization. In general, they are recommended for women who have already had children (because the cervix is less likely to expel the IUD). And because they have been linked to pelvic inflammatory disease (PID), which can lead to infertility, they are generally not recommended for younger women.	**98–99%**
SURGICAL METHODS, or sterilization, which are usually permanent and therefore not that popular with young people. For women, the procedure is tubal ligation, in which the fallopian tubes are blocked by being tied or clipped, making it impossible for sperm and egg to unite. For men, the procedure is vasectomy, in which the tube connecting the testes to the penis is cut and tied, so sperm are not released during ejaculation.	**99%**

On most college campuses, reproductive health counseling is available free of charge from the school's health office. Take advantage of this amazing service! College health providers can give you in-depth, confidential information about every available birth control method and help you decide which one is best for you and your partner. Do not be afraid to speak openly with a school doctor or nurse: These people are trained to deal with the specific needs of people your age, so they're very familiar with the emotional and physical aspects of college sex, and (in most cases) they are nonjudgmental people who will give you the straight scoop on sexual health and safety. Plan on visiting your school's health department whenever you have any questions or concerns about your health, and on going for regular checkups to help you maintain optimal sexual health while you're in school. One more perk: Because most college health insurance plans offer a discount on drugs, students can usually get affordable prescription birth control pills through campus health services or affiliated pharmacies.

Sexually Transmitted Diseases

STDs are extremely common in the US. More than 65 million Americans are currently living with an incurable STD, and 15 million more people become infected with one or more STDs each year—roughly half of whom contract lifelong infections. Between 20 and 25 percent of college students are or have been infected with an STD. One of the biggest problems with STDs is that they can be asymptomatic (meaning there are no visible signs of the disease), and people pass them on to their partners, who in turn may pass them on to even more people.

> **SAFEST SEX**
> The only safe alternative to barrier protection is to get tested for STDs at the same time as your exclusive partner, continue using barrier protection for six months after that (since it can take that long for certain infections to show up), and then get tested again to make sure the first test was correctly negative.

The most dangerous—that is, deadly—STD is AIDS, which is caused by infection with the HIV virus. The virus is transmitted from person to person through bodily waste, blood, semen, vaginal fluid, and breast milk. Women are particularly vulnerable to HIV infection during heterosexual sex. If a condom isn't used during oral sex, it's also possible that sperm cells carrying the virus can enter a woman's bloodstream through small cuts in her mouth.

The most common STDs among college students are chlamydia, HPV (human papillomavirus, a.k.a. genital warts), and genital herpes . Unlike HIV, most common STDs won't kill you, but they can leave you infertile and/or coping with lifelong symptoms.

Stopping the Spread of STDs The surest way to avoid spreading STDs is to practice safe sex with barrier protection—a condom, if it's heterosexual intercourse or oral sex performed on a man, and a "dental dam" or plastic wrap covering the vagina, if it's oral sex performed on a woman. Even if you know you're in a committed, monogamous relationship, you and your partner need to use barrier protection when you have sex to avoid the risk of swapping STDs that you may not even know you have.

STD testing is usually free and easy to do, and is always confidential as part of student health services, which often give away condoms and dental dams as well.

What to Do if You're Pregnant

Any time a sperm cell can meet one of your eggs, there's a chance you may become pregnant. Usually, it takes at least two weeks for tests to determine if someone's pregnant, so you may have to wait that long to get an official verdict. If your period does not come on schedule after unprotected sex, you should take a home pregnancy test (available at the drugstore) right away. If you want to double-check the results, you should then visit your school health office to take another test with a health care practitioner.

If it turns out you're pregnant, you will have to decide soon what to do:

If you decide to keep the baby, it's important to visit your school's obstetrician/gynecologist as soon as possible so that you can begin pre-natal care—which includes taking care of yourself in a way that's best for your baby's development. You will also have to think about how you will support

EMERGENCY CONTRACEPTION

If you have an accident with your normal method of birth control (such as noticing a hole in a condom after it's been used) or you were forced to have unprotected sex against your will and you're very certain that you don't want to become pregnant, you can take a form of emergency contraception known as the "morning-after pill." A large dose of hormones, which must be taken in two doses, twelve hours apart, within seventy-two hours of having unprotected sex, the pill creates changes in the lining of the uterus that make it inhospitable to a fertilized egg. For now, you can get a morning-after pill from your school's health services (or through a referral from the Emergency Contraception Hotline at 888-NOT-2-LATE), but because drug companies and pharmacists are agitating to sell it over the counter, women may be able to get it without a prescription soon.

and care for the baby once it's born. This is a major decision. Some women experience severe physical symptoms during pregnancy which will affect you (and maybe your ability to work) in the short term. More importantly, having a baby will affect you for the rest of your life.

If you decide that abortion is the right choice for you at this time, visit your school health department as soon as you can. (Abortions performed during the first three months of pregnancy are generally less physically risky.) There, you should be able to get a referral to a nearby health clinic or doctor who performs abortions. When carried out by a licensed, trained doctor in a sterile environment, the physical symptoms should only last for a few hours after the procedure, though the emotional aftermath can last substantially longer. For this reason, you may also want to talk to a counselor.

If you decide you don't want to have an abortion but aren't ready for a baby right now, you can give the baby up for adoption. Your school's health services office can refer you to state-approved adoption agencies in the area. If you do make the decision give up a baby for adoption, expect emotional repercussions.

Any decision you make will have a huge psychological impact, so it's a good idea to seek counseling regardless of the path you choose.

FOR RESOURCES ON PREGNANCY, ABORTION, AND ADOPTION, SEE P. 106.

Date Rape

Date rape is a very real phenomenon for college women. Many social scientists and law-enforcement officials believe that date rape actually occurs on college campuses much more often than it's reported, and that many female students fail to report it out of fear, embarrassment, and, often, reluctance to explain that drugs or alcohol were involved.

Date rape frequently occurs when the woman was willing to be sexual for a while, but then wanted to stop when the man became more aggressive. Talking about sex before the action starts—with a mutual statement of expectations—is one of the best ways to avoid such a predicament. But even if you do talk up front and you suddenly become uncomfortable with pressure from a man, no matter how far you've gone, you can and must tell him to stop in strong, unambiguous terms. "No," said repeatedly and firmly, will usually get your point across. If it doesn't, or you feel unsafe for any reason, leave—and don't worry about what your date (or other people) will think.

THE DATE RAPE DRUG

Rohypnol, a powerful sedative that's illegal in the United States, has become known on college campuses as the "date rape drug." By slipping the drug (also known as "roofie") into drinks, rapists use it to sedate their victims—often women they know. Complicating the prosecution of these cases, women who have been raped while under the influence of Rohypnol often have little or no memory of the experience—they wake up naked or in a strange bed and have no way of knowing exactly what's happened. Preventive measures: Don't leave your drink unattended at parties, and if someone you don't know well is pushing a drink on you, by all means take a pass.

WHAT TO DO IF YOU ARE RAPED

Don't immediately bathe, wash, or dispose of the clothes you were wearing before and after the attack—your body and clothing could provide important evidence for your case against your attacker.

Contact your school's rape crisis center. There, someone specifically trained to help people in your situation will be able to help you take the next steps.

Get to a health care facility as soon as you can. Your school's campus health service may be able to treat you with the standard rape kit procedure, in which evidence of rape (such as sperm) is collected. But if not, the campus rape crisis counselor can help you get to a clinic where the procedure will be possible.

In the weeks and months following a rape, get tested for STDs, pregnancy, and, six months after the attack, HIV infection.

Make sure you get the follow-up emotional support you need after a rape. It's common for people who've been raped to feel alienated from their friends who have never been through this kind of trauma, and talking to people who share your experience can really help speed the emotional recovery.

RESOURCES

College

Books

Barron's Profiles of American Colleges (Barron's Educational Series). Regarded by many as the college bible, this book offers detailed data on more than 1,650 American colleges and universities.

The Fiske Guide to Getting into the Right College by Edward Fiske and Bruce Hammond (Sourcebooks) offers well-organized information about schools (including best bargains, most innovative curricula, and subject specialties), how to apply, and how to foot the bill.

How to Write a Winning College Application Essay by Michael James Mason (Prima Lifestyles) offers detailed advice on how to structure and style your essay for maximum impact.

100 Successful College Application Essays compiled by Harvard Independence (New American Library) offers examples and analysis of 100 real essays on far-ranging topics that helped students earn admission to the colleges of their choice.

The Insider's Guide to the Colleges 2004: 30th Edition compiled and edited by the staff of the Yale Daily News (St. Martin's Press) provides a students' eye view of more than three hundred US and Canadian colleges, plus a thoughtful opening section advising students how to find an academic and social environment where they'll thrive.

On Writing the College Application Essay by Harry Bauld (HarperResource) is a classic, go-to guide on the art of crafting a great college-admission essay.

Web Sites

Collegiatechoice.com at http://www.collegiate-choice.com sells copies of video-taped tours to 350 US colleges.

College Visits, Inc., at http://www.college-visits.com, is a South Carolina-based company that conducts regular, regional trips to colleges for high school students in their junior or senior year.

Scholarstuff.com at http://www.scholarstuff.com provides links to websites and admissions offices of hundreds of colleges, plus links to numerous sites covering various aspects of college life.

Academics and Student Life

Books

The College Student's Guide to Eating Well on Campus by Ann Selkowitz (Tulip Hill Press). A well-informed nutritionist, Selkowitz advises students on how best to fuel themselves in all-you-can-eat cafeterias or the fast-food joints.

College Rules! How to Study, Survive, and Succeed in College by Sherrie Nist, PhD, and Jodi Patrick Holschuh, PhD (Ten Speed Press) is filled with practical advice on how to study hard and stay sane at the same time.

The Elements of Style by William Strunk Jr., and E.B. White (Pearson Allyn and Bacon). This clever classic will make paper-writing easier and more successful.

Majoring in the Rest of Your Life by Carol Carter (Farrar, Straus and Giroux) is a thoughtful, plainspoken primer on how to create a successful academic path through college and parlay that success into a rewarding career.

resources

Navigating Your Freshman Year by Allison Lombardo (Natavi Guides) offers helpful strategies for dealing with roommates, managing expenses, and many other student subjects.

Sex, Sexual Health, and Date Rape

National Organizations

Centers for Disease Control and Prevention
Address: 1600 Clifton Road NE,
Atlanta, GA 30333
Phone: 800-311-3435
Web site: http://www.cdc.gov

National Council for Adoption
Address: 225 North Washington Street,
Alexandria, VA 22314-2561.
Phone: 703-299-6633
Web site: http://www.ncfa-usa.org/home.html.

National AIDS Hotline: 800-342-AIDS

National STD Hotline: 800-227-8922

Planned Parenthood Federation of America
Address: 434 West 33rd Street,
New York, NY 10001
Phone: 212-541-7800
Web site: http://www.plannedparenthood.org

The Rape, Abuse, and Incest National Network (RAINN) is a nonprofit organization that provides free, confidential counseling twenty-four hours a day, from anywhere in the country, to people who don't live near a rape crisis center, as well as to those who might not know that they do live near a local center.
Address: 635-B Pennsylvania Avenue SE,
Washington, DC 20003
Phone: 800-656-HOPE
Web site: http://www.rainn.org

Web Sites

Go Ask Alice! at http://www.goaskalice.columbia.edu is a gold mine of answers to questions about sex, drugs, relationships, and emotional health.

Sexuality Information and Education Council of the United States (SIECUS) at http://www.siecus.org is a national nonprofit organization that provides information about sexuality and responsible sexual choices.

What If I'm Pregnant? at http://www.planned-parenthood.org/womenshealth/WhatifPregnant.html on the Planned Parenthood site addresses all options for pregnant women.

Books

The Go Ask Alice Book of Answers: A Guide to Good Physical, Sexual, and Emotional Health by Columbia University's Health Education Program (Owl Books). A great guide to all health matters, specifically geared toward college students.

Our Bodies, Ourselves for the New Century: A Book by and for Women by the Boston Women's Health Collective (Touchstone Books). A comprehensive guide to women's health.

Fraternities and Sororities

National Organizations

The National Interfraternity Conference
Address: 3901 West 86th Street, Suite 390,
Indianapolis, IN 46268
Phone: 317-872-1112
Web site: http://www.nicindy.org

The National Panhellenic Conference
Address: 3905 Vincennes Road, Suite 105,
Indianapolis, IN 46268
Phone: 317-872-3185
Web site: http://www.npcwomen.org

Web Sites

GreekPages.com at http://greekpages.com
provides information on fraternity and sorority
chapters at colleges across the country.

Drinking and drugs

National Organizations

Alcoholics Anonymous (AA) at
http://www.aa.org and **Narcotics Anonymous
(NA)** at http://www.na.org. Check the White
Pages or their Web site to find a chapter
near you.

The Center for Substance Abuse Treatment
at http://www.samhsa.gov/centers/csat2002/
index.html or 800-662-4357
provides information about various treatment
options.

**The Substance Abuse and Mental Health
Services Administration Substance Abuse
Treatment Facility Locator** at http://www.find-
treatment.samhsa.gov can help you locate
treatment in your area.

**The Higher Education Center for Alcohol and
Other Drug Prevention**,
Address: 55 Chapel Street,
Newton, MA 02458-1060
Phone: 800-676-1730
Web site: http://www.edc.org/hec/

Book

**Buzzed: The Straight Facts About the Most
Used and Abused Drugs from Alcohol to
Ecstasy** by Cynthia Kuhn (Norton) is a straightforward account of the most commonly used
drugs and how they affect the body.

Web Sites

The Task Force on College Drinking at
http://www.collegedrinkingprevention.gov is a
government-run site offering complete information about college drinking.

Sports

National Organizations

The National College Athletic Association at
http://www.ncaa.org offers news and information about college sports from basketball to
water polo.

Books

**The National Directory of Collegiate Athletics:
Women's Edition (College Directories)** offers
information about athletics at over 2,100
American colleges.

CHAPTER 5.

alternative education

Looking beyond traditional four-year colleges, there are a variety of specialized post-high school educational programs with many practical advantages—flexibility, affordability, and the power to fast-track people who already have clear professional goals into their jobs of choice. Technical and vocational schools, art and performing arts schools, community colleges, two-year colleges, associate degree programs, and apprenticeships that combine work with study are not new. But more and more jobs require specific technical skills and the working world has become increasingly transitory (requiring people to learn new skills every time they switch jobs). As a result, these alternative educational programs have surged in popularity, attracting students straight out of high school as well as older students in need of additional, highly focused education to advance their careers. If you are very directed in your goals and know for sure that you want to go into a specific field, a specialized school may make sense for you. While there are entire industries devoted to helping students get into four-year degree programs, there are fewer resources for people seeking alternative degree programs, so you must be more aggressive when it comes to researching.

The Occupational Outlook Handbook, the US Department of Labor's extremely thorough career guide at www.bls.gov/oco/home.htm, is a good place to find out what kind of schooling is recommended for almost any career you can think of.

Generally, alternative post-secondary schools and degree programs offer focused curricula designed to give students practical knowledge of the skills required for jobs in the fields of business, technology, health care, the trades, or graphic, visual, and performing arts. Typically at much less expense than traditional colleges and in two years or less, these institutions can prepare you for quite a few careers.

They can also get you started in any one of the thousands of other careers classified as "skilled labor" because they require technical and career education beyond a standard high school education, but not a traditional four-year college degree. Art and performing arts schools can run from two to four years, depending on the program and degree.

When you take a close look at today's work force and forecasted job trends, the benefits of alternative post-secondary schooling are strikingly clear. People with no education beyond high school are the most likely to be unemployed, and because jobs in "unskilled" labor are continuing to disappear as more and more everyday services are automated, the picture is only expected to worsen for them. But even a relatively short amount of schooling after high school gives people a remarkably big boost on the employment front. According to the US Bureau of Labor Statistics, more than half of the thirty fastest-growing occupations in the US—such as computer support and medical assistance (a field that's expanding to meet the increasing health-care needs of aging baby-boomers)—require some kind of vocational or technical training, rather than a four-year degree. And about 65 percent of today's jobs are skilled-labor positions, while only about 20 percent are "professional," requiring a college degree.

For people who've already figured out that they don't need a traditional college degree for the work they want to do—or who may not want to go down the college road right now—alternative schools can be a very good way to go.

SPECIALTY SCHOOLS (a.k.a. Technical Colleges, Trade Schools, or Vocational Institutes)

Vocational and trade schools are designed to teach people the interpersonal and technical skills they'll need to succeed in literally thousands of different fields:

FOR INFO ON HEATLH, SEXUAL HEALTH, AND OTHER ASPECTS OF POST–HIGH SCHOOL LIFE, SEE PP. 91–104.

electrical engineering **cooking** acuncture
midwifery RESTAURANT MANAGEMENT beauty
COMPUTER AND INFORMATION SCIENCE **martial arts**
technology **hotel management** personal **training**
music air-traffic control DENTAL HYGIENE
printmaking paralegal **fashion design**

They are usually highly specialized, offering intensive courses taught by academics and professionals who understand the latest advances and trends in a given field. Depending on the level of complexity of the work being taught, the degree and certification programs at these schools can be as short as two weeks or as long as two years.

Whether private or public, technical and trade schools tend to have strong ties to related industries and businesses in the communities where they're located—a big advantage at graduation time, since most vocational schools offer extensive job-placement services to their students. With so many adults changing careers numerous times, you will find many older students in these programs.

FOR INFO ON HOW TO FIND SPECIALTY SCHOOLS, SEE P. 130

Specialty schools might be a place you want to check out for a while to get certain training for skills you can use you whole life, even if you later decide to attend a four-year institution. There might also be training programs you can start while you are still in high school if your schedule permits and you are anxious to get a head start.

I love the hands-on experience that the college offers. (Canadian College of Massage and Hydrotherapy, NS, Canada)

I went to Technical and Further Education, studying art for six months, then media for six months. I loved that I was treated like an adult, and that the people in my classes were all different ages, so there was a maturity that wasn't there at high school. Plus we had guidelines that we had to follow for assignments, but then we could adjust them to suit us and put our own creativity into it, instead of being a clone making clone work.

SPECIALTY SCHOOLS

To give you an idea of the almost unbelievably wide range of nontechnological skilled trades you can train for, here is a list of miscellaneous specialty schools:

American Institute of Diamond Cutting (Deerfield Beach, FL)
Arques School of Traditional Boatbuilding (Sausalito, CA)
Brown Aveda Institute of Cosmetology (Mentor, OH)
California School of Herbal Studies (Forestville)
Culinary Institute of America (Hyde Park, NY)
New England School of Architectural Woodworking (Easthampton, MA)
San Francisco School of Piano Tuning (CA)
Seattle Midwifery School (WA)
Swedish Institute School of Massage Therapy (New York, NY)
United Bicycle Institute (Ashland, OR)
Wisconsin School of Professional Pet Grooming (Okauchee)

I went to a technical school to become a dental assistant. The good thing is that I'm doing something that I do well. But I would much rather be at the top, like the dentist.

I went to beauty school throughout high school, and got a job in a salon, but I hate doing hair and I learned the hard way. I'm gonna go to school for massage therapy, just to give me a better career name, and then one day I hope to go to school for psychology.

I'm going to school for culinary arts so that hopefully in the future I will be working in a four-star restaurant or a five-star hotel, and maybe a couple of years after that I'll have my own catering company.

I love that nursing school has an accelerated program, which means in two years I'll be done, while my friends are still getting deeper into debt in colleges and universities.

Caution!

As do other types of alternative schools, vocational institutes occasionally run scams, taking students' money in exchange for meaningless instruction and certifications that are virtually worthless on the job market. Beware of any promises from so-called degree mills that sound too good to be true—"Become a high-powered computer engineer in your sleep!"—and always make sure that any school you apply to is fully accredited by an independent accrediting agency, such as the Accrediting Commission of Career Schools and Colleges of Technology at http://www.accsct.org.

VISUAL AND PERFORMING ARTS SCHOOLS

Visual and performing arts schools teach highly specialized courses in a single discipline, or a range of closely related disciplines, in the fields of drama, dance, painting, crafts, filmmaking, and design, as well as just about any other creative discipline you can imagine. For people who've already discovered that their passions lie in the arts, they provide strongly focused, in-depth instruction and professional guidance that's helped launch many successful careers in the arts.

While many four-year colleges and universities offer degrees in the arts, there are quite a few schools that specialize only in these fields. While this total focus can be tremendous for your career, you will have fewer options for other fields of study. At many of these schools students will earn a Bachelor of Fine Arts (BFA), while others offer professional non-degree programs. Some schools specialize in one visual or performing art, while others are more generalized.

I was a freak in high school, but in art school I was very popular. I love being immersed in art and finally being around other people who understand art, and me! I love all of the other students, and it really feels like home. I hate that it is so difficult, and if you fail in art school, you're failing at something you've created and poured your soul into. It not only hurts your GPA, but it hurts your soul as well.
(Minneapolis College of Art and Design, MN)

I love that my college is so in tune with the real world. Also, the graduating percentage is very high, along with the minimum salary of its graduates. I will earn an associate degree in applied arts in graphic design. I liked that there was a type of art that could be executed in the digital medium.
(Art Institute of Dallas, TX)

I enrolled in the Advanced Writing Program at the Institute of Children's Literature. I love to write and the writing program has really helped me with the business side of writing.

The beauty of Pratt is its size, with all classes capping off at around 20-25 students. Everyone's guaranteed individual attention—and serious training (don't expect to splash some paint on a wall and call it a day). Pratt's foundation art and architectural programs are among the most rigorous available.
(Pratt Institute, New York, NY)

SPECIALIZED VS. GENERAL EDUCATION

Because many artistic disciplines can be pursued in liberal arts colleges or universities, it's worth considering the pros and cons of going to a specialized school. Being almost exclusively surrounded by other artists can provide a very stimulating environment—most everyone you encounter at an art school will be able to relate to some aspect of your work and/or life as an artist. Many artists find they work well in this situation and appreciate the open discourse about art that it can provide.

On the down side, art schools can be competitive (although the same can often be said for specialized departments within other schools—or, for that matter, any environment where many people have the same goal in life). It's also true that the same things that make art schools so focused can make them limiting. While most art schools provide the opportunity for (and many even require) students to take classes outside of their primary area of concentration, these courses are usually not the main strength of the institution.

So if you're an artist of some kind and are considering your next move after high school, you'll need to weigh these factors and think about what's more important to you immediately and in the long term—diving directly into your creative interest with the greatest possible focus, or getting a more well-rounded education.

HOW I GOT HERE

Parsons had been my dream school. I had read about two girls who went there, graduated, and went to Paris, and then Elizabeth Taylor and Richard Burton opened a boutique for them. And I thought, "OK, all I have to do is go to Parsons." When I reread the story as an adult, I realized it was Mid Fonssagrives and Vicki Tiel. I hadn't understood that Mid was [model] Lisa Fonssagrive's daughter and her stepfather was [photographer] Irving Penn. As a kid you don't see the connections that lead to things. You just see going to Parsons, then graduating and going to Paris. So that's how I decided to go to Parsons.

ANNA SUI,
FASHION
DESIGNER

ART AND DESIGN SCHOOLS

Whether your talent lies in documentary filmmaking, arts and crafts, or cutting-edge computer graphic design, you can acquire valuable professional skills through certification programs at the following nationally recognized art and design schools (just a sampling):

I went directly to an art school. I loved it and the people were so cool! I was designing clothes, learning new techniques, drawing and perfecting my craft every day! I also liked the creative writing and English classes. I LOVED every moment . . . I now have my own company. I am doing very well selling my art and clothing!

SOME WELL-KNOWN ART SCHOOLS

The Anthropology Film Center (Santa Fe, NM)
The Arrowmont School of Arts and Crafts (Gatlinburg, TN)
Art Center College of Design (Pasadena, CA)
The Art Institute (located in 30 major cities across North America)
Atlanta College of Art (GA)
Boston Architectural Center (MA)
California Institute of the Arts (Valencia)
California College of Arts and Crafts (San Francisco and Oakland)
Center for Creative Studies (Detroit, MI)
The California School of Professional Fabric Design (Berkeley)
Cleveland Institute of Art (OH)
Corcoran College of Art and Design (Washington, DC)
The Fashion Institute of Technology (New York, NY)
Maine College of Art (Portland)
Maryland Institute College of Art (Baltimore)
Massachusetts College of Art (Boston)
Memphis College of Art (TN)
The New York Studio School of Drawing, Painting, and Sculpture (New York)
Pacific Northwest College of Art (Portland, OR)
The Penland School of Crafts (Penland, NC)
The Pilchuck Glass School (Seattle and Stanwood, WA)
The Pratt Institute (New York, NY)
Rhode Island School of Design (Providence, RI)
School of the Art Institute of Chicago (IL)
The Skowhegan School of Painting and Sculpture (Skowhegan, ME)
Southern California Institute of Architecture (Los Angeles)
University of the Arts (Philadelphia, PA)
University of Cincinnati School of Design, Art, Architecture, and Planning (DAAP) (OH)

If you want some training as a self-sufficient filmmaker, San Francisco State offers schooling for aspiring filmmakers in the cutthroat society of motion pictures. (San Francisco State University, CA)

PREPARING YOUR PORTFOLIO

Since every school has different admission requirements and emphasizes different techniques and disciplines in their training, it is essential to check in with the admissions department of any school you're applying to, in order to see what they specifically look for (and require) from prospective students. But here are some general guidelines to think about as you prepare your portfolio.

Showcase your observational skills. In most artistic disciplines, translating what you see with your eyes into your work is key, so include some pieces that demonstrate your ability to capture the essence of real objects and people.

Demonstrate your keen sense of composition. In painting, graphic design, or any other field of the arts, the way you compose an image is extremely important. Make sure that the pieces you include in your portfolio convey your ability to use the page in a considered, eye-catching way.

Think about themes. If you do tend to focus on specific subjects in your work, let that shine through. Part of being a good artist is having ideas, and your choice of subject matter factors into how people see your work.

Be original. While schools may have different opinions about what kind of content they are looking for, imagination is almost always an asset. Your ability to reproduce other people's work will never make as much of an impact as your ability to create your own.

Send in your best work. Though there's some debate about whether it's better to submit a consistent portfolio or one that includes pieces in a wide variety of styles and media, all art school admissions officers agree it's best to include what you know to be your very best work—no matter what style it's in.

SOME OF THE MANY THINGS YOU CAN STUDY IN ART AND DESIGN SCHOOL

Advertising

Computer Arts

Fashion

GRAPHIC DESIGN

Illustration

INDUSTRIAL DESIGN

Interior Architecture and Design

Motion Pictures and Television

Photography

Fiber Arts   ANIMATION

Painting

Cinematography

I went to the High School of Art and Design [in New York], where I studied photography. There were a few people there who wanted us to go into filmmaking. I really didn't know how you went about getting trained for that. When I started looking into film schools, it was very limited, and I couldn't afford to go to school and also go across the country. I was limited to New York, and there were only two places: the School of Visual Arts, and NYU.

[In college] my whole life revolved around money: how I was going to get it, how not to spend it. I was jealous of people who could just go to school and live with friends in the dormitories. I could not afford to be concerned with the social life and the material things that many teenagers have and want. I never really felt like a teenager.

I just knew I wanted to make movies. When I was in film school, it was just so arrogant to say you wanted to direct, and then when I got to the American Film Institute, they would give us material to direct, and I knew I hated that. We were told: "Here's three pages from *Bell, Book, and Candle.* Direct it." And it was like, "Er, maybe I don't want to be a director." I just wanted to make my own little movie.

AMY HECKERLING, FILMMAKER

HOW I GOT HERE

PERFORMING ARTS SCHOOLS

If you are 100 percent sure that you want to pursue a career in the the performing arts, here are some reputable performing arts schools where you can specialize in acting, dance, or music.

DANCE SCHOOLS

Ailey School (New York, NY)
Lou Conte Dance Studio (Chicago, IL)
School of American Ballet (New York, NY)
Joffrey Ballet School (New York, NY)
Atlanta Ballet Centre for Dance Education (GA)
Ballet Idaho Academy (Boise, ID)
Dance Theatre of Harlem School (New York, NY)
School of Dance Connecticut (Hartford)
Pacific Northwest Ballet School (Seattle, WA)
Martha Graham School of Contemporary Dance (New York, NY)
Merce Cunningham Studio (New York, NY)
Juilliard School (New York, NY)

DRAMA SCHOOLS

American Academy of Dramatic Arts (New York, NY and Hollywood, CA)
American Musical and Dramatic Academy (New York, NY and Hollywood, CA)
Dell'Arte International School of Physical Theatre (Blue Lake, CA)
Juilliard School (New York, NY)
Larry Moss Studio (Los Angeles, CA)
Lee Strasberg Theatre Institute (New York, NY and Los Angeles, CA)
Neighborhood Playhouse School of the Theatre (New York, NY)
New World School of the Arts (Miami, FL)
Stella Adler Academy of Acting and Theatres (Los Angeles, CA)

MUSIC SCHOOLS

Academy of Vocal Arts (Philadelphia, PA)
Berklee College of Music (Boston, MA)
Boston Conservatory (MA)
Cleveland Institute of Music (OH)
Curtis Institute of Music (Philadelphia, PA)
Juilliard School (New York, NY)
Manhattan School of Music (New York, NY)
New England Conservatory of Music (Boston, MA)
Old Town School of Folk Music (Chicago, IL)
San Francisco Conservatory of Music (CA)
VanderCook College of Music (Chicago, IL)
Wisconsin Conservatory of Music (Milwaukee)

I love jazz music so I wanted to go to a music school. At Berklee I can sing while walking down the halls and people join in instead of shunning me.
(Berklee College)

AUDITION TIPS

Every performing arts school is looking for something different in its applicants, so be sure to research carefully every school's admission requirements. Then, bear in mind the following strategies to make sure your audition goes as well as it possibly can.

Be prepared. If you're required to play a song or perform a dance or monologue for your audition, make sure to research and memorize your lines/steps completely beforehand—it's the best way of increasing your confidence.

Show up early. That way, you'll have a few minutes to sign in, get the lay of the land, and relax before your audition.

Take several deep breaths to steady yourself before walking onto the stage.

Ask (politely) if you can begin again if you make a mistake.

Thank the admissions panel for their time after your audition. Being personable and professional will always make you a more attractive candidate.

COMMUNITY COLLEGES (a.k.a. Junior Colleges)

Like small universities, two-year community colleges typically offer students a wide variety of liberal arts courses and a range of on- and off-campus extracurricular clubs and activities. Originally designed as public institutions that could provide transitional education between high school and four-year colleges, they continue to be excellent "springboards" for students who choose to live at home (or on their own) and/or improve their academic standing before going on to transfer to four-year colleges. Those students not interested in attending a four-year college can instead complete a two-year associate degree at most community colleges.

Over the years, to meet growing demand for specialized education, community colleges have started offering vocational training in addition to traditional liberal arts courses. Many have developed strong ties to local businesses—an invaluable asset for students looking for work, before and after graduation. And a fair number of community colleges have earned national reputations for excellence in their areas of vocational specialization. (The program in performing arts at Miami-Dade Community College, in Florida, and the program in digital animation at Santa Monica College, in California, are just two examples.)

Although most community colleges do not provide campus housing, their relatively intimate scale and motivated student bodies make their classrooms and cafeterias lively places where it's possible to connect with people of different ages and from different backgrounds. As at every kind of school, classes in popular departments tend to fill up quickly at community colleges, so savvy students need to keep an eye out for new course listings and registration dates and make an effort to connect with professors early to express their interest in joining certain popular classes. But students generally praise their teachers' energy and the unpretentious academic environment of community colleges.

I really like the fact that it's local, but at our local facility there aren't many extracurriculars.
(Lincoln Land Community College, Springfield, IL)

I wanted to go somewhere local, where I could get my basics in before transferring to a bigger, more expensive four-year university.

One more important piece of good news about two-year colleges: Since most are part of state and city public university systems, their tuition is typically a fraction of that at traditional colleges. And since many community colleges now have what are known as "two-plus-two" transfer arrangements with both public and private four-year colleges, it's possible for someone to attend a community college for two years, build up her GPA if need be, then finish the last two years of college at the four-year school. Students taking advantage of two-plus-two programs end up graduating with degrees from the four-year schools but without having paid higher tuition for the full four years. (Two-plus-two programs are so popular that a few technical institutes are beginning to offer them, too.)

A lot of graduating seniors think that they NEED to go to a four-year university when they don't. I saved a lot of money and time going to a career college and I'm graduating one-and-a-half years earlier than most of the people I graduated with.
(Baker College, MI)

My first college semester was spent in dorms at a bigger state school, and it was a bad experience. I like a small, commuter-school setting, where students and professors/faculty take it seriously. It's a great transfer school. People make successful transfers to bigger four-year colleges, which is what I plan to do.
(Cape Cod Community College, West Barnstable, MA)

Going to community college is allowing me to:
1. boost my GPA
2. mature and appreciate my education
3. gain scholarships to transfer to a reputable four-year school.
(Westchester Community College, Valhalla, NY)

Distance Learning

Formerly known as "correspondence education," when students took assignments and returned homework by mail, "distance learning" is the new term for coursework completed in pursuit of a certificate or associate's degree outside the classroom. With the remarkable telecommunicating flexibility now provided by the Internet and high-speed modems, it's become a red-hot nontraditional educational option. Distance learning is almost exclusively conducted online these days, with students and teachers interacting through a variety of computer and video conferencing programs. Some distance-learning courses allow students to work at their own pace (so long as a course is completed within a certain time limit), while others require students to adhere to traditional classroom schedules— that is, to be logged on and in attendance at the same time every week.

Distance learning is obviously not ideal for people who prefer the familiar, face-to-face dynamic of a traditional classroom. But for self-motivated people interested in pursuing college degrees while they work or honor other commitments, distance learning is an extremely attractive option at an affordable price. The popularity of distance learning has risen sharply as people on one end of the continent realize they can take classes from colleges on the other end without ever leaving home (or giving up their day jobs). The US Department of Education estimates that there are now about two million online students involved in one form of distance learning or another, and the National Center for Education Statistics has reported that nearly one-third of all colleges and universities now offer some form of distance learning.

Schools offering distance learning have different enrollment requirements. Some will let people join their virtual classrooms as soon as they've paid the fees, while others require proof of academic performance, as well as an application essay, to enroll (much like traditional colleges). When researching distance-learning programs, it's important to find out exactly what type of computer and modem you will need and whether or not you'll be able to access the schools' online

> I was doing and still am doing my courses over the mail and computer. I like being able to take an exam with nobody breathing down your neck and in my PJs.

digital libraries and/or other resources, such as a career-placement office. (Many schools provide students earning distance degrees with toll-free phone numbers, so they can speak to instructors and other campus personnel at no cost.) Because some shady online "universities" are now, unfortunately, marketing fake distance-learning degrees, it's also extremely important to make sure that any institution you're considering taking online classes with has been accredited by one of the six regional accrediting agencies that verify the merit of all academic programs.

FOR A LIST OF THE WEB SITES OF THE SIX NATIONAL ACCREDITING AGENCIES, SEE RESOURCES ON P. 126.

ALTERNATIVE-DEGREE SCHOOLS

1. **Obtain applications for admission from the schools' Web sites or by calling the schools directly.**

2. **Submit the relevant application forms to your high school guidance counselor** to make sure she or he sends your high school transcript (including your test scores) directly to the schools you're applying to.

3. **Follow all instructions on the application carefully.** Most technical and trade schools have rolling admissions policies, which means that you'll usually receive an admission decision back from the school within four to six weeks of application, and, if you're admitted, that you'll be eligible for enrollment at the start of the next semester.

MAKING IT HAPPEN

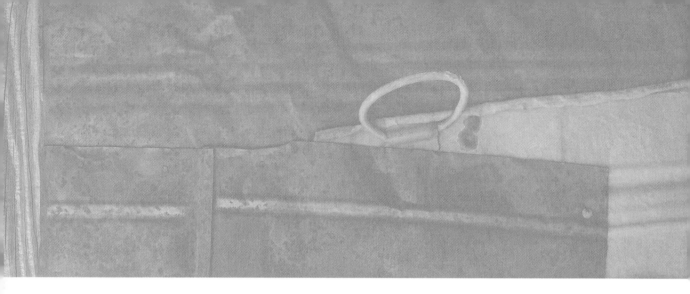

Apprenticeships

A number of the skilled trades, such as carpentry, cooking, and electrical science, offer formal apprenticeships through local unions, which you can ordinarily learn about through your state's employment or apprenticeship agencies. But it's also possible for you to become an apprentice by informally approaching someone you admire and offering to assist them in their work—stretching canvases, sweeping out a metal shop, peeling carrots, or performing similarly unglamorous tasks in exchange for exposure and experience. Following a tradition that's been around for centuries, apprentices generally start with low-level positions in their chosen field and receive hands-on instruction from veteran workers as they advance from menial to more complicated tasks. Occasionally, apprentices attend supplementary classes at trade or technical schools to round out their education. One big advantage of apprenticeships—formal or informal—is that they offer people the chance to "earn while they learn," since apprentices usually take home a wage as they learn a trade. The other advantage is that apprentices who've proven their abilities during their training are frequently offered permanent positions at the companies where they've apprenticed, or placed with similar companies by the unions they've trained under.

I am currently apprenticing at a spa to become a full esthetician and to do other stuff related to the field such as massage therapy, etc. I love the people I work with and the atmosphere I work in.

Cooperative Training/Work-Study

A modern cousin of apprenticeships, cooperative training programs, now offered by many vocational schools and two- and four-year colleges in the US, allow students to combine work with study in a variety of formats. Typically, co-op students earn credit and pay for the part-time work they perform at companies (including many in the Fortune 500) who've agreed to partner with local colleges. Cooperative college programs either combine work and study during the same semester (with students usually spending about two-thirds of their time in the classroom), or students work full-time one entire semester, then study full-time the next.

As with apprenticeships, the odds that graduates of cooperative programs will quickly find jobs in their chosen fields are high: The National Commission for Co-op Education estimates that about 80 percent of co-op graduates have no trouble landing jobs after graduation, either at their co-op companies or with companies looking for the same skills they've learned on the job. The success of co-op education hinges on the fact that it gives students a chance to apply what they've learned in the classroom in a real-world work environment, and therefore to graduate with impressive resumes and references.

RESOURCES

Specialty Schools

Books

You're Certifiable: The Alternative Career Guide to More Than 700 Certificate Programs, Trade Schools, and Job Opportunities by Lee and Joel Naftali (Fireside) delivers the lowdown on a multitude of training programs for such diverse occupations as Feng Shui consultant and hot-air balloon pilot.

Peterson's Guide to Vocational and Technical Schools (Peterson's Guides) provides in-depth information on thousands of accredited US post-secondary educational programs, in two volumes: East, covering schools east of the Mississippi, and West, covering schools west of the Mississippi.

Organizations

The National Accrediting Commission of Cosmetology Arts and Sciences provides a list of accredited cosmetology schools.
Phone: 703-600-7600
Website: http://www.naccas.org

The National Restaurant Association can help direct you to schools and other information related to the food industry.
Phone: 202-331-5900
Web site: http://www.restaurant.org

Web Sites

Peterson's IT Channel, at http://www.petersons.com/itchannel, offers a searchable database of Information Technology programs and jobs, as well as info on computer based training resources and certification.

Visual and Performing Arts Schools

Books

The Performing Arts Major's College Guide by Carole J. Everett (Arco) provides specialized college advice with sections on dance, drama, and music, including audition tips and rankings for performing arts programs.

Peterson's Professional Degree Programs in the Visual & Performing Arts (Peterson's Gudies) is an exhaustive listing of programs throughout the country.

Organizations

The National Office for Arts Accreditation is the umbrella organization for four separate groups that accredit all art and design, theater, dance, and music schools across the country.
Phone: 703-437-0700
Web site: http://www.arts-accredit.org

Web Sites

Peterson's Visual and Performing Arts at http://www.petersons.com/vpa has a database you can search by program type or name, as well as articles about specialty schools.

Art Schools.org at http://www.artschools.org, offers an extensive school list through which you can browse or search to learn quick facts about each school, and contact them through the site.

Community Colleges

Book

Two-Year Colleges (Peterson's Guides) is a large compilation of two-year programs.

Web Sites

Juco.com at http://www.juco.com is a site dedicated to promoting the academics and athletics at junior, technical, and community colleges.

Distance Learning

Book

The Official Guide to Distance Learning by Shannon Turlington (IDG Books Worldwide) is an in-depth, instructive guide to the pros and cons of distance learning.

Web Sites

The Distance Education and Training Council at http.detc.org accredits distance-learning and vocational schools everywhere in the US.

eCollege at http://www.eCollege.com provides information about online programs available at two hundred schools.

The following six regional school accrediting agencies are responsible for accrediting schools in the states over which they have jurisdiction:

Middle States Association of Colleges and Schools: http://www.msache.org

New England Association of Schools and Colleges: http://www.neasc.org

North Central Association of Colleges and Schools: http://www.ncacasi.org

Northwest Commission on Colleges and Universities: http://www.nwccu.org

Southern Association of Colleges and Schools: http://www.sacs.org

Western Association of Schools and Colleges: http://www.wascweb.org

Apprenticeships and Cooperative Education

Books

The Uncollege Alternative: Your Guide to Incredible Careers and Amazing Adventures Outside College by Danielle Wood (ReganBooks) is a funny, frank guide to jobs you don't need to go to college for.

But What If I Don't Want to Go to College? by Harlow G. Unger (Checkmark Books) outlines the professional advantages of non-college learning programs.

Organizations

The US Department of Labor, Employment Training Administration's Bureau of Apprenticeships and Training can put you in touch with numerous skilled-trade apprenticeships and other job-training programs in your area.
Phone: 877-US-2JOBS
Web site: http://www.doleta.gov

Wider Opportunities for Women offers information and training resources for women interested in pursuing nontraditional jobs.
Phone: 202-464-1596
Web site: http://www.wowonline.org

Web Sites

National Commission for Cooperative Education at http://www.co-op.edu is an excellent source of information about cooperative education programs.

The **Vocational Schools Guide** at http://www.vocational-schools-guide lets you search for schools by state or degree program. You can do the same for technical schools with the **Technical Schools Guide** at http://www.technical-schools-guide.com.

work

People go to work after high school for various reasons:

to gain some financial independence

to pursue a dream career

to subsidize an education

or simply to bide time until they figure out
what they want to do next.

A job can be a brief, meaningless blip on your journey, or it can become a major turning point in your working life. Sometimes it's hard to know in advance where one job may lead you. But it can't hurt to know what you'd like to be getting out of your work.

Before you embark on a job search, it's important to figure out what you want to get out of work, and what you might be best suited for. Answering the following questions can help you to target your search.

ask yourself

>> **What do you want out of work? Money, experience, or something else?**

>> Do you want to work full-time? Part-time? Days? Nights? Weekends?

>> **Do you like working with people or on your own?**

>> What type of environment do you feel most comfortable in? A retail store? An office?

>> **Did you dream of having a particular job when you were a kid? If so, how does your childhood plan sound to you now? Have your goals stayed the same, or have they changed?**

>> Have you ever heard about a job that sounds totally interesting and fun to you? Which aspects of that job are most intriguing to you?

>> **What, under any circumstance, would you not do for money?**

>> Where do you see yourself in five years?

Supporting Yourself

People think about work, at any stage of life, in different ways. For some, work is a life calling. For others, it's just a temporary way to make money. Depending on where you are in life, and what your goals are, your approach to finding and keeping a job will vary.

Life costs money. While families provide differing levels of support to their children as they grow up, many are unable (or unwilling) to continue financial support beyond the boundary of high school graduation. And some people would rather move straight to a state of financial independence. There are a number of reasons people look for money-making work straight out of high school.

I worked retail—both the biggest mistake and best choice of my life. I loved that I got to interact with a lot of people, and that I got a paycheck that I could spend on anything I wished. Customers treat retail workers [poorly], retail managers treat workers [just as bad], the hours are long for relatively low pay, and the jobs don't involve any brain stimulation whatsoever—I'm the type of girl that needs to be challenged.

I was a third grade literacy tutor for an AmeriCorps program. I loved that it was already possible for me to get a "non-grunt" job, a job where I could use the talents I had to actually accomplish something, rather than just helping some company make money by doing something anyone else could have done. I had a hard time dealing with the kids—I had to be as much a negotiator and disciplinarian as I was a teacher.

Your RIGHTS in the Work Force

As a hardworking wage earner, you need to make sure your rights are respected in the work force. The US Department of Labor's website at http://www.dol.gov provides up-to-the-minute information on all federal rules and regulations relating to work, although it is always important to check with your state's labor bureau, since regulations can vary by state. Here are some federal legal employment standards that you should be aware of.

Minimum wage. Under the Fair Labor Standards Act, workers are entitled to a minimum wage of $5.15 per hour.

Breaks. Under federal law, employers are not required to give employees breaks; however, when employers do offer employees short breaks (between five and twenty minutes), those breaks should be paid. Lunch breaks of thirty minutes or more do not need to be paid.

Pay raises. The federal government does not mandate yearly raises, but, as a matter of standard practice, your employer may offer annual raises at a rate that you should be made aware of when you begin work.

Sick leave. The federal government does not require employers to pay for employees' sick leave. However, the Family Medical Leave Act entitles employees to up to twelve weeks of unpaid leave for family medical reasons (such as giving birth to a child or caring for an ailing parent).

I went and looked for a job and I got one as a check-out chick. I didn't really love it, I just did it for money. Since then I've gone back to college. It is much better, because now I will be able to further my education to get a better job.

I took a year off before college to figure out who I was. I got a job, moved out, and tried to make it on my own and live my life the way I wanted to. I learned who I was and proved to myself that I could do it. I also proved my parents wrong—they thought I wouldn't go back to school and would end up living back with them, but I did register for school this year and am still on my own and living for me!!!!

I tried to experience life on my own, to have a little knowledge of what I'd be doing once I left for college. My family was still close. I also got a job. I hated the "I told you so" when I admitted it wasn't as easy as I thought it would be.

I moved away from home, got a very well-paying job, and got my own place. I am currently working and trying to get my college schedule to work around work. I hate having so many money problems but I do like having the freedom of my own place.

I was doing odd modeling jobs ever since I started high school. By the time I graduated, I had offers from two modeling companies and I joined one of them. The year after graduation, I started working full-time as a fashion/advertising model.

It was glamorous and fun. I love the looks on people's faces when they see me all geared up; it gives me confidence to walk into the room and know that all the people there are waiting for me. All the traveling is pretty cool too and I get to have freebies from whatever company I'm promoting. I've continued my modeling career but I try to make it part-time sometimes so I can continue my courses. I've started fashion design and international relations because I know that modeling doesn't last forever. The good thing is now I have a higher value of myself and a better hope for my future (after twenty-five) and the bad part is, well, there is more work to be done and I seldom have any time left for other things.

I worked at a car dealership for two years after high school. I was working nonstop, wondering where I'd be if I went to school . . . I didn't even have any real motivating interests then . . . I hated not knowing where I would be in ten years . . . I still don't know. I'm only twenty and I'm as confused as you all are, too.

My boyfriend got into a bad car accident in March of '03, and since then—it's now July—I have been taking care of him and doing some serious soul-searching . . . I realize life is really fragile. Everything can change in a heartbeat. I am now planning to go to school in fall of 2004 to become a nurse, because of my boyfriend's accident. It taught me a lot about being an RN, and how much you affect people's lives.

I wasn't sure whether I wanted to go to college or work. So I figured I'd take a year off and work. So that's what I've been doing this past year—working. When I was in school, if I didn't feel like going or was sick I'd just roll over and go back to sleep. But with work, you can't do that; if you take too much time off it looks bad. I've finally decided that I want to further my education. I'll be starting classes part-time this fall, just trying to take it one day at a time.

I got a job the summer after I graduated. As August rolled around, I decided to move down to Florida, because that was where I was wanting to go to college. So I moved and found a nice house and job before I started to attend college in the spring. I had a lot more freedom than my friends; I didn't have to study and I could go out and have fun, just do whatever.

I took a road trip from North Dakota, where I lived, to New York City, and got involved with a few small acting jobs while waiting tables. I've stayed in New York with some new friends of mine. I continue to wait for a big movie role, but I'm getting there. I love the fact that I continued to persevere and that I'm getting closer and closer to my goal.

Supporting Your Dream

Another reason to work for money is if the work you really love does not pay well, or only pays sporadically. As generations of starving artists can attest, careers like painting, writing, and pottery making are not always lucrative in the early stages. And so to support themselves, people interested in artistic endeavors like these have to find work that gives them enough money to live on but doesn't take up too much of their time or leave them too tired to pursue their calling in their spare time. If you think you are going to need to have the job for a number of years, choosing a job with financial growth is important.

If you'd like to dedicate time to projects that may be more about love than money, it's a good idea to figure out when you do your best work. If you like to write during the morning when everyone else in your house goes to the office and it's suddenly quiet, you might look for a high-paying nighttime job, such as waitressing or tending bar in a restaurant or club. But if your creative juices start flowing in the evening, you might prefer to find a day job that won't sap too much energy.

HOW I GOT HERE

I remember when [the YMCA] switched my shift to 7:30 in the morning [from 5:30 a.m.]. That may have been one of the happiest moments of my life.

When I got into the resident company [at Second City], I remember thinking two things: one, that my name would go on the wall with the list of all the perfomers, and two, that I would get health insurance.

I think if you ask any of us here, we all dreamed of ending up on *Saturday Night Live*. I remember thinking, I'll just keep doing this as long as I can get away with it. My parents are cool with me studying drama; I'll do that. Oh, I got on Second City. I'll just keep doing this until they won't let me do it anymore, and then I'll get a real job.

TINA FEY, COMEDIAN/WRITER

I got a job as a dancer at a Houston gentlemen's club, mostly because I needed the money for rent and to pay medical expenses. I live with my boyfriend, who is great. I am working on getting my writing published and fronting a band. I also got my bartending license as a backup plan, just in case the dancing didn't work out.

I went into small-time acting, while my dream is to be a big-time actress. I had to work night shifts at a restaurant as well, something I vowed I'd never do. It was a new beginning for me. A small chance to prove myself and go my own way. I was glad to at least have a shot at making my dreams come true . . . It was so different from what teachers tell you to expect. They almost make it sound like you'll find an employer on your doorstep—you have to go find one yourself. I'm still working hard on my career. For all those out there wanting to go to Hollywood, it isn't easy—but never quit. I've had to move to a little apartment and I have a crappy car; that's the bad part. The good part is that I know if I keep trying I can go somewhere and make it count.

Temping—signing up with a temporary employment agency that will assign you to long- or short-term jobs in understaffed offices—is one of the best ways to earn good wages during the day, and it's been a life-saver to many artists. (To temp, you'll need to have good interpersonal skills and know how to type, but a college degree usually isn't required.) The big advantage of temping is that it allows people to work steadily for a couple of weeks or months, then take as much time off as they need to focus on their creative work.

I started a band. It's called Freak-o's. It's a band that consists of all my friends. I also work part time at Burger King.

HIGH-PAYING JOBS YOU CAN GET WITHOUT A COLLEGE DEGREE

Bartender

BUILDING MANAGER OR SUPERINTENDENT

Carpenter

Construction worker

House painter

Nanny   Personal shopper

Chef

Taxi Driver

Working for Experience

If you have a pretty good idea of what you want to do with your life (at least for now), you may feel eager to find a job right away that will enable you to begin acquiring skills in your chosen field. You might be able to find an entry-level position without a college degree and decide that's what you want to do—working full-time or working part-time while you earn a degree, using your income to help pay for school. But before going this route, it is important to figure out if you will ultimately need a degree or some other kind of education to advance in this field and, if so, to begin thinking about where and when you'll get the education you'll need to succeed (unless you would be comfortable in an entry-level position indefinitely).

Another good reason to work for experience is to connect with people who share your interests. If your career goal falls into the not-so-lucrative category, you might want to look for a day job in an organization that's connected to the work you love to do in your spare time. Say you want to be an actress and you're taking acting classes at night—you might consider looking for work in a theater. In this case, your day job might include such mundane tasks as stitching torn costumes or typing the names of prospective donors into a computer, but you'd probably learn a great deal from this behind-the-scenes experience and enjoy the company of like-minded coworkers. And who knows? You might find that a career in theater administration or costume making is something you want to pursue long-term. Or just maybe you'll make some critical connections with good people involved in the acting world that will provide you with opportunites in that field.

I found a job as a teacher's aide at a day care. I loved that I could find out if I really wanted to be a teacher at a day care and what age group I wanted to work with. I didn't want to study for something I might end up not really wanting to do for the rest of my life.

I worked in construction for three years, then went to college because I now hate construction. It's not easy being a girl in construction!

I took a little bit of time off to just sit back and think about what I wanted to do with the rest of my life. In January, I got a full-time job and now I am making a very comfortable living and deciding what I want to do to continue my education.

I loved the fact that I didn't rush into college. I can't count the number of people I graduated with who rushed off to college and have already dropped out or transferred or switched majors because they didn't take enough time to relax and think about their next move.

INTERNSHIPS

An internship is a temporary, unpaid position (or a position paying only a nominal wage) specifically designed for a person who's eager to learn the ropes in a certain field. Because internships provide people with basic introductory information about jobs—as well as that first, all-important experience in a given profession—they can be extremely helpful career stepping stones. Many college and graduate students seek out internships in fields like biology, law, publishing, and just about every profession in between, which are designed to complement their fields of study. Often, internships take place during the summer, when it's possible to get a concentrated dose of work experience between semesters. But many students—including high school students—work as interns part-time during the school year. For some, interning can be an alternative to a more formalized education.

While interns in understaffed offices are occasionally given as much responsibility as full employees, interns are often assigned tasks that aren't very glamorous—filing, answering phones, tallying receipts, making photocopies, and the like. Many internship programs are well established and competitive (such as those in government offices in Washington, DC, for college students interested in working in government after they graduate), but others are less formal. Since many college and high school guidance offices establish

The Art of Interning

Be personable. From the moment you show up for your first interview, make eye contact with your prospective employer, ask well-informed questions that will demonstrate your honest interest in learning as much as you can about the job, and, above all, be yourself. Conveying energy and enthusiasm, as well as your sense of humor, will make your bosses more eager to have you around, and therefore more likely to invite you to work closely with them on interesting projects.

Be picky. If you don't feel any chemistry between you and a prospective employer during an internship interview—or the prospective employer is taking pains to emphasize that your job will be 100 percent drudgery, with very little interaction with the rest of the staff—don't be afraid to say "Thanks, but no thanks." You'll most likely be able to find another employer looking for an intern, who understands that even a minimal amount of mentoring is invaluable to you and a small price for them to pay in exchange for your free labor.

Be industrious and professional. If your fellow interns are sitting around doodling while they wait to be given more work, don't follow suit. Find a batch of papers you can organize or some envelopes that need to be addressed—or better yet, check with your supervisor to see what needs to be done. The more you prove your willingness to work hard, the more likely it is that you'll be given bigger projects.

Be alert. While some of the material you're xeroxing or stuffing in envelopes may be confidential, which means that you shouldn't discuss it with anyone outside of the office (and it's always best to assume that it is confidential, unless your boss tells you otherwise), make a point of reading what's in front of you. Keep your ears open to office chatter. Don't be afraid to ask a lot of questions. Even the most mundane-seeming document or discussion can help you understand the business better.

internship programs for students with alumni working in interesting jobs in the community or across the country, you may be able to find an internship through your school's career guidance department. Or you may be able to create your own internship position by approaching someone whose work interests you—one of your parents' friends, a neighbor, or even someone you find in your local yellow pages. Sometimes, letting someone know you want to learn all you can about what they do and proposing the kind of position you'd like (professionally and politely, of course) is all it takes to earn the title of intern.

If you're lucky enough to have the kind of internship that gives you broad exposure and responsibility, the experience can give you a good idea of whether or not you really want to pursue a career in the field. It can also teach you administrative and communication skills that will help you in almost any job (entry-level or otherwise) you'll have in the future. But even a seemingly sleepy internship—in which you become intimately acquainted with a Xerox machine—can still be worthwhile if your supervisors are willing to answer questions and talk to you about their work: how their days are normally struc-tured, how the business or agency finds and keeps its clients, and, ideally, how the reams of material you're xeroxing fit into the big picture. Just being in the office gives you an opportunity to see how things work and get a better idea of whether you're interested in pursuing a particular road further. The best way to go into an internship is always with a positive attitude, determined to get as much as you can out of the experience. But it's also important to feel confident that your supervisor, in exchange for your hard work, will take time to educate you on the fundamental ins and outs of the business. The clearer you can be with a supervisor about your own goals when taking an internship, the more you will benefit.

Many Emersonians intern with Boston news-papers, film companies or television studios. The Princeton Review has voted Emerson's radio station number one in the country.
(Emerson College, Boston, MA)

FOR MORE ON COMBINING INTERNSHIPS AND OTHER ENTRY-LEVEL POSITIONS WITH SCHOOL, SEE P. 138.

VOLUNTEERING

There is never a shortage of organizations, institutions, and businesses that would be thrilled to take on enthusiastic volunteers. If you don't need the money, could use the experience, or simply want to help out in an area that's interesting or would really benefit from your contribution, volunteering can be a terrific and fulfilling opportunity. Since you're working for free, odds are, whatever you take on will be flexible. And because you're giving of your time and talents, the people you work for are unlikely to dump on you (for fear of losing their free help). They'll probably try to give you interesting tasks. The best reason of all to volunteer: It's good karma.

I volunteer once a week at a used-book shop whose profits go to the Bryn Mawr scholarship fund, which isn't much but it's good to get away from class and kids my own age and deal with dust and back-cramping filing work and old people. Plus, Patsy allows me to take a book home with me after every session, so I save tons of money that I would otherwise have been spending on the books I so desperately need to keep my eyes from glazing over from an excess of schoolwork.
(Yale University, New Haven, CT)

GETTING YOUR FOOT IN THE DOOR

There is a huge upside to getting a foot in the door of the kind of company you'd ultimately like to work for. Many employers eventually end up hiring their former interns for full-time jobs. But there are other ways to make a favorable first impression with a prospective employer aside from interning with them. Contacting the employer (or anyone at any level who works where you'd like to work) for an informational interview, volunteering with the organization you're interested in if it's a nonprofit (such as Planned Parenthood or the American Cancer Society), and applying (repeatedly, if necessary) for grunt-work-only entry-level positions at the company with the intention of working hard to prove your talents are all good ways to demonstrate your interest and natural competency.

I volunteer at a local hospital. I find it fulfilling because I feel good about helping out.
(Pasadena City College, CA)

Career counselors say that the best way to find a job, even in economic downturns when many companies are hiring less than usual, is to make yourself known to employers as a person of exceptional drive. Your efforts to wedge your big toe through a tiny chink in the employer's front door may not succeed immediately. But if you're patient and persistent, it's more likely that you'll come to mind when the company is ready to hire.

Working and School

Some people go the route of school and work if they need to contribute to the cost of education or cover their expenses while they're in school. Other students opt for jobs or internships that will complement their studies and put them in a good position to find fulfilling full-time work when they graduate.

SUPPORTING YOUR EDUCATION

If you don't have a work/study job as part of your financial aid package, you can find a part-time job with flexible hours that will allow you to schedule day and night shifts around your academic schedule to help cover your expenses during the school year. Another option is to spend your summer vacation working longer hours. Seasonal labor jobs are typically both easy to train for and abundant when the weather's warm. Outdoor summer work can be physically demanding, but it can help students stockpile enough cash to keep them flush during the school year. Answering newspaper help-wanted ads, regularly checking job listings posted in your school's career office, and pounding the pavement (filling out applications and dropping your resume off at places that are hiring) are all reliable ways of landing work. But in today's tight job market, it's a good idea to explore employment options as widely as you can—with as much help as you can get—through the process of networking.

I'm a clerical assistant at John Deere health care. I like it because it has flexible hours. I go to school full-time and I don't really have a choice. I'd do better in school if I didn't work, but I need the money.
(Blackhawk Community College, Moline, IL)

I work at a day care. It teaches me a lot about how differently kids can react in the same situation. It also teaches me how to deal with adults, because if they don't like something that happened at the day care, you have to know the right things to say to them.
(Kirkwood College, Cedar Rapids, IA)

I took a year off from school and got a job bartending in New Orleans, LA, on Bourbon Street. It's something I have wanted to do for a while. It's exciting and challenging, because I'm so young. Plus it pays very well—after a couple of months, I had enough money to pay for my whole tuition for school, which would have been a problem if I hadn't taken the job.

I waitress. It brings in good money. I've worked since I was fourteen; no biggie.
(College of Dupage, Glen Ellyn, IL)

Flexible jobs you can hold down during the school year

After-school or foreign-language tutor for children

Babysitter

BARISTA AT A LOCAL COFFEE SHOP

Home health-care aide for an elderly person

HOUSECLEANER

Restaurant hostess

FOR MORE INFORMATION ON WORK-STUDY, SEE P. 123.

High-paying jobs you can do during your summer vacation

Carpenter

CONSTRUCTION WORKER

Golf-course caddy

Lifeguard

Swimming instructor

VENDOR AT AN OUTDOOR SUMMER FESTIVAL

Making it Happen:

WORK

THE ART OF NETWORKING

1. **Make a list of every single person you can think of who's involved with work that interests you.** Your list should be as long and diverse as possible, including your parents' friends (and their friends), your friends' parents, names your guidance counselor gives you, and people you may not know personally but have seen in action in your community or your school. (This is why it's important to attend any and all career fairs or conferences offered at your school: The people who participate in these programs have already agreed to make themselves accessible to students, so it's a pretty safe bet they'll be more than willing to help you in your job search if you reach out to them.)

FOR MORE ON NETWORKING, SEE P. 32.

Even people outside of your immediate environment can be helpful if you can find a way of reaching them.

2. Pick up the phone and contact everyone on your list.

After finding out whether or not the person you've called has a few minutes to talk to you (and phoning back at a later, agreed-upon time if he or she was too busy when you first called), explain that you're trying to find a good job and what you think your skills are. Ask the person to tell you what their own job is like (what the work involves, what skills it particularly requires, and what they most enjoy about it), and if they can recommend any other people you might call. The idea behind networking is not to put pressure on the people you call by asking them if they can hire you themselves. Instead, you want to convey that you're open to all interesting opportunities and eager to work hard as you learn the ins and outs of any specific job.

(A note of encouragement: Cold-calling people can be scary. But try to remember that most people love to talk, and most people reeeeeally love to talk about themselves. There's a chance that someone you contact may tell you straight out that they can't be of any help. Don't take it personally, and don't be discouraged. Just move on to the next name on your list. More often than not, the people you reach out to in the course of your networking will be flattered that you've taken an interest in them and likely to take an interest in you in return.)

3. Follow up by calling all the people whose names you were given during the first round of calls.

This is how your web of contacts becomes a true network: one connection sparking one more, or maybe six more, and so on and so forth. In the process of networking, you'll get a clearer picture of what's involved in a wide range of occupations. And if you follow up on each lead with your expanding pool of knowledge about the working world, you'll increase your chances of finally reaching the person who's been looking (consciously or unconsciously) to hire someone just like you.

> I wait tables. It's really taught me how to communicate better with people. I'm quite shy.
> (University of Las Vegas, NV)

4. Be yourself, in professional mode, at any informational or actual job interview.

If one of your network contacts agrees to meet you for a face-to-face informational interview or, better yet, invites you to come in for an actual job interview at their office or workplace, be sure to show up on time and properly attired. (If you're not certain of what to wear, just ask the person interviewing you about their dress code.) And above all else, be yourself. Answer the questions you're asked honestly, rather than how you imagine they're supposed to be answered. And don't be afraid to ask all the questions you really have about the job. That's the only way you'll both know whether you're the right person for the position in question.

5. Keep the faith as you search.

Looking for a job can be incredibly stressful, especially if you've hit a few dead ends in row. But that's why it's important to take regular breaks from your search: See your friends, get plenty of exercise, and consider volunteering as a way of connecting with others and maintaining confidence in yourself as you forge ahead with your job search. You may need to take a part-time temporary job to keep money coming in as you look for full-time work in the field you're really interested in. But try to remember that job-searching is a game of skill, luck, and endurance—and the more you expand your network, the greater the likelihood that you'll land a great job.

Working and going to school is really hard. I have been struggling to maintain my grades while supporting myself.

Starting Your Own Business

If you've got the next **big** idea, a terrific one-of-a-kind product, or a clever and much-needed service to offer, you might think about starting your own business. With a bit of ingenuity, some business savvy, investment capital (though not necessarily a huge amount), and a whole lot of drive, you can become a successful, self-employed business owner.

FINDING YOUR NICHE

The first step in creating your own business is to identify your skills and what it is you want to do (or produce). Maybe you're interested in setting up a traditional freelance business, such as a catering business or graphic design firm. Or perhaps you've invented a healthy, tasty sandwich that will revolutionize the fast-food business. In both cases, you'll need to do some marketing research to find out how and where to set up shop to attract the most business and see your dream become reality. Reading about successful business ventures and their founders' experiences can also be very valuable as you try to find your own way.

To see how other people feel about your idea, you'll need to survey the public. Does your proposed business seem to satisfy a long-standing need in the community, or would it be redundant? Does it make sense from a geographical, economic, or even aesthetic point of view? By distributing questionnaires to people who congregate in the neighborhood you're thinking of locating to, or even by going door to door, you can find out if your idea is original enough, or makes enough common sense, to fly.

I opened up a pet grooming shop. I love being with animals at all times, but I hate only having one day a week off . . . and only two weeks of holidays a year . . .

DEVISING A BUSINESS PLAN

Once you've determined your business has potential, you'll need to come up with a business plan. A business plan is a document that contains a comprehensive description of your business—including budgets and goals. The plan can help you to make decisions about your business

I started my business designing clothes, jewelry, and shoes. I loved that my ideas were out there and people were finding out what my ideas were. I loved that people got to see what I loved, and I didn't have to hold back.

I've been launching my business. I have a new line of clothes that should hit the department stores in the early fall of 2004. I love my life right now, because although I am on my own and have to deal with my problems on my own, I am doing it myself, and being independent.

I wrote for anything that would accept my writing, because it's my passion. I liked not having a full-time or stressful job. I hated that I did not have a steady income.

goals, as well as potentially attract investors. In writing your plan, you'll need to decide if you'll be the sole proprietor of your enterprise (which would give you plenty of freedom but also total financial responsibility), or whether you'd prefer to go into business with a partner or partners (which might mean less financial responsibility, but also less control and possibly more emotional tension, if you and your partner can't see eye to eye).

When you're ready to put your plan into action, you'll need to find space to set up your business and purchase any equipment you might need to get you up and running. You'll also need to figure out how much work you can handle at any given time. (Since you'll be relying on customers to spread the word about your reliability from the get-go, you'll need to fulfill your very first orders with aplomb.) If you can't handle it alone, you may need to look into hiring employees, which will make your business more complex.

PROMOTING YOUR NEW BUSINESS

Small business owners often say that the thing they like most about their work is that it lets them (or, actually, forces them to) wear many hats—becoming mathematicians, scientists, copywriters, or art directors, depending on the day's tasks. Creativity—combining your artistic, verbal, and maybe even

HOW I GOT HERE

I realized that although I was working on projects that were $20 billion in size [at the White House], nothing had happened in four years. I needed to run something that I owned and that I could make my own decisions with . . . It [the store that became the Barefoot Contessa] was love at first sight. I had no idea at the time how to run a business or how to buy food whole-sale, but I knew this was for me."

INA GARTEN, OWNER OF BAREFOOT CONTESSA, BESTSELLING COOKBOOK AUTHOR

HOW I GOT HERE

At 16, we sold cosmetics door-to-door. During college, [at Indiana University] we gave makeovers in a sorority house. Jane graduated with a degree in business, and I graduated with a degree in fine arts. Jane ended up doing some retail thing, I painted murals then worked my way up to becoming the training director for Clnique. Eventually, we decided to open up our own makeup store. This was in 1976, the height of the women's movement when no one wore makeup and people thought we were nuts. We went to San Francisco's Mission District where a lot of Latin women, who traditionally love color and makeup, lived. We were sort of an overnight success.

JEAN DANIELSON AND JANE FORD, CREATORS OF BENEFIT COSMETICS

I was never qualified for any job I had. I always learned on the job. I didn't know anything about business before I started with *Forbes*, and I didn't know anything about stocks when I moved to Wall Street. Once on the job I did learn a lot.

I had a lot of successes, but what really made me fearless was my complete failure at Ziff-Davis [where she was hired to start a newspaper, which flopped]. Once you've lived through that, you know you can survive, and you're not as scared. Everybody should have a real failure, ideally when they are pretty young, that gives them a sense of confidence . . . There's nothing to build confidence like real achievement, but also like real failure.

Genuine achievement gives you a sense that you can do stuff. And genuine failure gives you a sense that you can survive being imperfect. Because the delusion that you're perfect—or that if you just do the right thing, things will always work out OK—makes you resistant to change and fearful of failure.

ESTHER DYSON,
PRESIDENT,
EDVENTURE
HOLDINGS

theatrical skills—is absolutely essential when it comes to promoting your business. To attract customers, you'll need to tell them what's unique about your business and what special needs it fulfills. And then you'll need to come up with eye-catching ads, posters, and special giveaway offers to bring in business.

Another important way to promote your business is by getting out into the community and meeting with people who might be able to send work your way. For instance, if you're going into graphic design, you might make an appointment to speak with the manager of a local copy shop to show samples of your work. That way, when a customer comes into the copy shop looking for help designing a Web page or party invitation, the copy shop (assuming it doesn't do that kind of work itself) might be willing to refer the customer to you. Establishing personal contacts and strategic alliances—in which proprietors in related fields recommend each other's services in a you-scratch-my-back-I'll-scratch-yours exchange—is critical to the success of small businesses. Running your own business might require you to spend a lot of hours by yourself, but it will also put you in touch with many new people—your customers and fellow entrepreneurs. And it's this kind of variety in day-to-day work life that energizes and inspires many self-employed small business owners.

HOW I GOT HERE

I graduated from high school at sixteen. I was fascinated with tattooing and spent most of my time reading books about it and talking to popular tattoo artists. I also met my current boyfriend, who was eighteen at the time and also a tattoo artist. He became a great source of information for me. I started working in a tattoo parlor as soon as I could, after I turned eighteen, and I hope to start my own shop one day.

I went to college for a few semesters just to experience it, then left to buy half of our family's insurance agency when my dad's partner left for another job. Since I have my own business, it's a big responsibility, and an even bigger one to know that my clients depend on me to tell them what kind of protection they need.

A great way to learn more about entrepreneurship is through Junior Achievement, a national organization designed to put young people in touch with established business owners who act as their mentors. For information on local chapters of JA, consult the national website at http://www.ja.org.

Committing your business plan to paper

After you've done some serious thinking about how your business will operate, whom it will serve, and how much the whole operation is going to cost, you'll need to write all this information down and distribute it to potential investors (i.e., Mom, Dad, Bill Gates, that nice little old lady down the street whose lawn you've been cutting for years, or anybody else who you think might want to help you realize your dream). To make them eager to get in on the ground floor, you need to include the following:

An attention-grabbing description of the highly creative merchandise or service you plan to offer.

A detailed explanation of how and why your merchandise/service is unique, and filling a clear need in your community.

A clearly organized, step-by-step plan for setting up your facilities and marketing your merchandise/service.

An honest estimate (based on well-documented research) of the funds you'll need to get your business off the ground. This includes all of your expenses, including goods, any overhead costs (such as rent and salaries—including your own if you plan to take one).

Military Service

With roughly 350,000 new recruits signing up each year, the combined armed forces—the US Army, Navy, Marine Corps, Air Force, Coast Guard, and their reserve components (such as the Reserve Officers' Training Corps, better known as ROTC)—are the single biggest employer of young people in America. And there's no doubt that a stint in today's technologically advanced, highly specialized military can provide valuable training for many different types of work—ranging from engineering to health care to transportation to trumpet playing—and many other financial and career-building advantages.

In addition to basic pay, free room and board, medical and dental care, paid vacations, and more, military personnel can earn college credit for training they receive on duty, which can help them earn associate's degrees from community colleges affiliated with branches of the military (such as the Community College of the Air Force). Alternatively, service members can earn tuition assistance for up to 75 percent of the cost of college courses taken at other local colleges or through correspondence programs during their off-duty hours. Under the new Montgomery GI Bill Program, military personnel can put aside money from their monthly pay to help cover the cost of future education once they're out of service, and each branch of the military provides veterans with additional contributions toward education.

Making a career in the military has handsome benefits, too. Since military personnel are able to retire with a pension after twenty years, many veterans are grateful for the chance to stop working and relax in midlife, or to embark on a new civilian career with a degree of financial security.

But for the obvious reason that all types of enlisted personnel (who make up 85 percent of the military) and their supervising officers (who make up the other 15) can be sent into combat or to war-torn parts of the world to support frontline fighters, military service can also be much more dangerous and morally challenging than other types of work. As a famous recruitment slogan once put it, life in the army (or any branch of the military) "is not just a job; it's an adventure." But if you're thinking of signing up for this particular adventure, it's very important to weigh the pros and cons carefully with your family and friends and make sure you know exactly what you're getting into.

UNDERSTANDING THE TERMS OF SERVICE

Typically, people wanting to enlist must sign a legal agreement saying they'll commit to eight years of service. Depending on the terms of the contract, fifteen months to six years are spent in full-time active duty and the rest is spent in the reserves. (Reservists can re-enter school or a civilian job, but they may still be called back for military service should the need arise.) Prospective recruits for each branch must be US citizens or resident aliens and pass a physical and a written examination, known as the Armed Services Vocational Aptitude Battery.

Much like the career tests described in Chapter 1 (see page 6), the ASVAB helps recruiters find out which military occupational training programs enlistees might enjoy and qualify for. If you are thinking of military service as a means to an end—a way to raise money for a college education, say, or to acquire particular technical skills—it's important to know what kind of training is required for the type of civilian job you'd eventually like to have. With that in mind, you should then be able to figure out if a specific military occupational training program will give you the skills needed for your dream career, and whether or not you'll still need additional training for that career after you leave the service.

Since taking the ASVAB does not in any way obligate you to sign up for military service, you should feel free to take the test, look over your results, and discuss all of your enrollment options with a recruitment officer in any branch of the military you're interested in, without feeling pressure to make an immediate decision. Recruitment officers are typically well informed and frank, when pressed, about all aspects of military life, but since their job is primarily to recruit, keep in mind that they may emphasize the most alluring aspects of life in their branch. It's also important to note that the

ROTC

The Reserve Officers' Training Corps is a selective program designed for people who wish to make a career in the military. ROTC offers college students the chance to train in army, navy, air force, and marine units while earning undergraduate degrees at various colleges and universities across the country. On top of their regular courses, ROTC trainees take two to five hours of military instruction a week.

During the last two years of the program (typically an ROTC student's junior and senior years of college), students receive a monthly allowance. After graduation, they may serve as officers in the Armed Forces for a predetermined period of time. ROTC also offers generous scholarships on a two-, three-, and four-year basis to exceptional students.

I decided to join the army to pay for college. I loved being a part of a group. I hated being told what to do.

armed forces—which make no bones about requiring a high level of personal sacrifice, physical and emotional endurance, and an attitude of "embracing the suck" from members—do not make it easy for recruits to quit. Occasionally, military personnel are discharged for serious medical reasons, or family hardship. But in general, second thoughts and cold feet (especially in times of war) don't get a lot of sympathy from commanding officers. Joining the military is a very big decision—and also one that usually can't be undone. So be sure to take plenty of time to discuss what you've learned about your options in the military with your family and any friends or relatives with military experience before making your final decision.

WOMEN IN THE MILITARY

Unfortunately, sexism and a certain amount of macho aggression are facts of life in the armed forces. Despite recent efforts to crack down on sexual misconduct and make the armed forces more hospitable to women—who make up approximately 20 percent of annual recruits—female recruits can still encounter mild to severe forms of sexually charged harassment. In May 2003, the Defense Department Inspector General's survey found that nearly 20 percent of female cadets said they had been victims of sexual assault. Seven percent said it was in the form of rape or attempted rape. However, the military's rules and commitment to promoting on the basis of performance (when applied correctly) can create a professional environment that's unusually hospitable to women.

Women are eligible to enter most military specialties and, like their male colleagues, they can train to become mechanics, missile maintenance technicians, and fighter pilots. But for now, women are generally barred from direct combat. Because women can't prove their talents in combat, this does create a barrier for military women who might like to advance their careers to the highest ranks.

MAJOR DECISION

A big part of keeping the peace between nations is the fact that one (or both) sides in any dispute has tanks, ships, and planes ready to do battle if necessary—the mere idea that these forces could attack is sometimes all it takes for nations to find a way to resolve their conflicts without violence. But if you are considering military service, either as a way to train yourself for other careers or as a career in and of itself, you do need to decide how you feel about the worst-case military scenario: the prospect of being required to participate in or support actions that might result in death. Some people believe that there are occasions when it's necessary to go into battle to protect certain freedoms or liberate people from oppressive rulers. But other people believe that governments should always seek nonviolent, diplomatic means of international problem solving. Only you can decide what you think about war—and peace, love, and understanding, for that matter—but it's extremely important to figure out what your own beliefs are before signing up for military service.

I joined the United States Air Force as a jet mechanic. I loved being able to tell people that! Plus, I knew I was doing something to help my future. I would have a steady paycheck, get to see the world for free, and get to further my education for free. Plus, it fills me with pride to know that my mother is so proud of me. But I had to leave all of my friends and family, and I lost a lot of my freedom, too. Plus, there is nothing easy about Basic Military Training.

I plan to finish up my four years here, and get the schooling to become a teacher.

I decided, wow, I want to fight for my country and make a difference. So I decided to join the military. I loved that I was standing up for my country and all that I believed in. I also loved that I was fighting for the good guys in the war. I am trying to get higher and higher in my position in the military and hope to make a difference.

I joined the United States Marine Corps while I was still in school and left for boot camp the summer after high school. It was a challenge. All my other friends just hung out and stayed at home, living off their parents. Now I'm completely independent, traveling the world and learning new things. I feel like I can accomplish anything after boot camp.

I'm now in Pensacola, Florida, attending school for aviation electronics. I enjoy being in Florida and enjoy the nice weather. It's hard because I had to leave my family and friends behind and a life in the Marine Corps is so unpredictable. But then again, that's what makes it exciting. I also plan on getting my associate degree for architecture while on active duty.

RESOURCES

Internships

Books

Choices for the High School Graduate: A Survival Guide for the Information Age by Bryna J. Fireside (Ferguson) is packed with information on after–high school internship, apprenticeship, military, and national and international volunteer work opportunities.

The Internship Bible (Princeton Review) offers information on more than 100,000 internships in various fields, as well as interviews with famous former interns.

The National Directory of Arts Internships (National Network for Artist Placement) provides listings for internships in various arts-related fields, including museum and gallery work, film and video, and performing arts design.

Web sites

The Fund for American Studies, in partnership with Georgetown University, at https://www.dcinternships.org/index.asp provides information on summer and semester internships in government and business in Washington, DC.

Idealist.org at http://www.idealist.org/ provides a link to international non-profit internships.

Inroads at http://www.inroads.org/ helps place minority students in corporate internships around the country.

Magazine Publishers of America at http://www.magazine.org/internship/ helps college and graduate students find internships in the publishing industry.

Starting your own business

National Organizations

The American Woman's Economic Development Corporation is a nonprofit organization dedicated to training and counseling women entrepreneurs at every level of business ownership.
Address: 216 East 45th Street, 10th Floor, New York, NY 10017
Phone: 917-368-6100
Web site: http://www.awed.org

The National Association of Women Business Owners is a member organization that helps women business owners strengthen their professional and political power.
Address: 8405 Greensboro Drive, Suite 800, McLean, VA 22102
Phone: 800-55-NAWBO
Web site: http://www.nawbo.org

The Small Business Administration is the government's extremely helpful resource and information center for small-business owners.
Address: 409 Third Street SW, Washington, DC 20416
Phone: 1-800-U-ASK-SBA
Web site: http://www.sba.gov

The U.S. Department of Labor Women's Bureau provides a wide range of information for women interested in starting their own businesses or pursuing nontraditional occupations.
Address: Frances Perkins Building, 200 Constitution Avenue NW, Washington, DC 20210
Phone: 800-827-5335
Web site: http://www.dol.gov/wb/

Books

Kick Start Your Dream Business: Getting it Started and Keeping You Going by Romanus Wolter (Ten Speed Press) offers motivation and encouragement as well as tips on how to start a business.

Start Your Own Business: The Only Start-Up Book You'll Ever Need by Rieva Lesonsky and the editors of *Entrepreneur* magazine (Entrepreneur Media) covers a lot of stuff (so nothing's covered in great detail), but is a good, easy-to-read overview.

The McGraw-Hill Guide to Starting Your Own Business: A Step-By-Step Blueprint for the First-Time Entrepreneur by Stephen Harper (McGraw-Hill) offers advice about keeping a small business afloat, as well as pointers on how to start one.

The Young Entrepreneur's Edge: Using Your Ambition, Independence, and Youth to Launch a Successful Business by Jennifer Kushell and Steve Mariotti (Random House) addresses the concerns that are unique to younger business owners, like how to gain the respect of older clients and how to have both a business and a life outside of it.

What No One Ever Tells You About Starting Your Own Business: Real-Life Start-Up Advice from 101 Successful Entrepreneurs by Jan Norman (Upstart) is a collection of stories from entrepreneurs who have started businesses and lived to tell the tale.

Web Sites

Young and Successful Media at http://www.youngandsuccessful.com offers a place for young entrepreneurs to meet, network with, and find support from others in the same situation.

High School Start-Ups at http://www. highschoolstartups.com is geared toward teens thinking of starting a web-based business.

Military Service

Books

Absolutely American: Four Years at West Point by David Lipsky (Houghton Mifflin) is a fascinating, behind-the-scenes look at life at the elite military service academy.

In the Company of Men by Nancy Mace (Simon and Schuster) tells of the author's grueling battle for respect as one of the first woman graduates of the Citadel.

Jarhead: A Marine's Chronicle of the Gulf War and Other Battles by Anthony Swofford (Scribner) is a gripping, politically-charged autobiographical account of a former marine sniper's experience fighting in the first Gulf War.

Web sites

Careersinthemilitary.com at http://careersinthemilitary.com is the central information source for the US military, with a list of thousands of military careers and information about all five branches of the armed forces.

Todaysmilitary.com at http://todaysmilitary.com is the US Department of Defense's detailed site designed to educate young people and their parents about careers and day-to-day life in the armed forces.

CHAPTER 7.

travel

So you'd like to see the world, travel abroad, or check out a distant corner of the US you've always been curious about. You may find that your bold plan will make some career-minded people nervous, since they'll worry that present or future employers will regard your wanderlust as a sign of reluctance to buckle down to life's serious business. But you'll find plenty of others—fellow explorers, educators, parents, and employers—who understand and appreciate the horizon-expanding, confidence-building advantages of travel. And these people will probably tell you the same thing: Go for it.

As it happens, more and more people are now opting to spend time after school traveling, studying, or working someplace new. For students who feel burned out after packing their high school schedules with extracurricular activities in order get into competitive colleges, deferring enrollment for a year of travel is a good way to rejuvenate after graduation—and get the most out of an expensive education when they do arrive on campus. (At Harvard, where letters of acceptance have long encouraged students to take time off before coming to the university, the number of students who chose to defer almost tripled in the last decade). And for students who may not have gotten into the college of their choice, spending time gaining valuable skills and experience in a new environment often improves their applications the second time around.

Travel takes you away from the familiar, exposing you to new people, cultures, and ideas—but in a funny way, it also helps you learn about yourself. And if you still need to convince any skeptics, you might want to point out to them that colleges and prospective employers very often look favorably at applicants whose life experience pops off the page. What better way to test your mettle and distinguish yourself from the pack than, say, helping build a school in Africa, working at a raptor rehabilitation center in Alaska, or perfecting your French working at a hotel in the south of France? You'll probably be proud of yourself for seeing and surviving someplace you've never been before, and the ingenuity and imagination it took to get you there may ultimately impress other people, too.

If you're interested in traveling, there are literally thousands of ways to go about it. You'll need to think seriously about where you'd really like to go, what you'd really like to do, and how you'll finance your own unique journey. But the time you spend carefully planning your trip will be worth it, because chances are it will challenge and change you in ways you'll relish the rest of your life.

I went to all different places around the world. I really thought it would be a good way to expand on my views and my life values. I love the fact that I lived not knowing where I was going to be the next day. Also trying to understand the people and their ways of life. I have been getting up every day and living life to the fullest because that is what I learned when I traveled.

I went with a couple of my friends and traveled around Central and South America. I loved seeing the different sights and different cultures in all the different countries.

I have only two suggestions for anyone reading this. 1) Don't go to college and get a job and tie yourself down right after high school. You'll be doing it the rest of your life, so why start now? When you're young, you've got to go out and explore, express yourself, learn, meet people. No one's gonna do it for you. 2) Don't plan. Relying on fate can be tough; it's not for the weak. But it makes for the most interesting, fun, and extraordinary experiences EVER!

TRAVEL

As soon as I graduated high school, I sold or gave away all my unnecessary possessions, packed my things, and traveled through Europe. No maps, no tours, no schedules. I just gathered together all my money and left, placing my life in the hands of fate.

Much as you might network in search of a job, make a list of everyone you know (or have heard about through friends) who spent time traveling after high school or while in college. Then contact them and try to find out what their experiences were like. Would they plan their trips exactly the same way if they could do it again today? And if not, what would they change about their trip and why?

Do you have a specific destination in mind? If you know others who have visited places you'd like to see, get in touch with them. Inside tips from people who have been there can really improve your travel experiences, and expose you to things you might otherwise miss.

Contact any national or international travel or work programs that sound interesting to you for informational brochures and application materials. Most well-established international programs—such as Rotary International (at http://www.rotary.org) and the National Outdoor Leadership Schools (at http://www.nols.edu)—have their own Web sites, but you may end up having to write directly to a few overseas programs to request information.

Find a way to finance your journey. If you want to work on a volunteer service project abroad, you may only need money to cover transportation to and from that country. There are also opportunities to work overseas.

Get a passport. Duh. If you're planning to travel abroad, you're going to need one of these. You can pick up application forms at many local post offices or download application forms on the US State Department's Web site (http://travel.state.gov). To get your first passport, you'll have to apply in person at an authorized US post office; a federal, state, or county courthouse; or one of the passport agencies around the country. (The State Department Web site can steer you to whichever is closest to you.) You'll need to bring a 2-by-2 inch photo of yourself, proof of your US citizenship (such as a certified birth certificate), and a check, money order, or credit card to pay the processing fees. (Currently, the total fee is $85 if you're sixteen or over.) Passports usually take six weeks to process, so be sure to apply for one far enough in advance of your trip.

Get a visa if need be. Check with the consulate or embassy of any country you plan to visit to see if you need special permission to work or study while you're there.

Safeguard your health and safety. As soon as you know where you want to go, consult the State Department Web site to find out if there are any security warnings about travel to the country or countries you'd like to visit. And make sure to visit the Centers for Disease Control's travel health information service (at http://www.cdc.gov/travel/) to find out about any shots you may need to get before visiting foreign countries, and how to protect your general health while traveling abroad. Before any trip abroad, it's always a good idea to visit your doctor and dentist for checkups to reduce the likelihood of unexpected medical emergencies.

I had been traveling. Travel was like a university without walls, and I picked up many ideas on rituals of the body. Years later, it began with a little shop, mostly based on traditional ideas and products that I'd seen on my travels. We used the cheapest bottles we could find. We hand-wrote our labels because we couldn't afford to have them printed. This frugal approach actually became a sort of DNA for us. That was really how it started—in a little shop. Then everything exploded...

ANITA RODDICK, FOUNDER, THE BODY SHOP

HOW I GOT HERE

I flew across the country by myself to Seattle, WA. Then I flew to LA, and then drove to a small lake in Spokane.
Discovering strengths in myself I didn't know existed, and learning how to cope with weakness, are things you can't learn from a college textbook.
I travel still, and I have learned how to pack a decent bag, make my way through airports, and chat up complete strangers. I've met so many friends from my travels, and it just makes life so complete-feeling.

TRAVEL SAFETY

Because a number of overseas terrorist attacks have directly targeted American tourists, tourist spots (such as hotels and clubs), and government agencies abroad, it is extremely important to understand the risk of terrorist attacks. To help travelers protect themselves, the US Department of State provides frequent country-specific travel announcements and general public warnings at http://www.travel.state.gov. Before you leave home, it's a good idea to read and print out addresses and contact information of the US consulates in every country you plan to visit. In general, you should plan on contacting the consulates in case of emergency. But in the event that a terrorist attack targets a US consulate, or some other nearby concern, you should obviously keep your distance until you receive information from local police and/or health authorities, who can help steer you to assistance set up for American travelers abroad.

TRAVEL

Exploring On Your Own

Solo travel is undeniably exciting, often leading to unexpected adventures with unlikely comrades. But that's also, frankly, what can sometimes make it stressful and dangerous—especially for people who aren't familiar with the local language or customs, and especially for women. For this reason, it's important to do as much research as you can to educate yourself about the countries or areas you'll be visiting before you leave home, and to consider traveling with a friend (at least for part of your journey), so you can look out for each other while you're on the road.

I got a job for awhile, just an easy job working at a juice bar, and continued driving my younger sister to high school, living at home, and using my spare time to take hiphop classes and do activism work. When I'd gotten enough money together, I bought a plane ticket and flew to Germany. I just had to indulge in some curiosities I've always harbored before diving into a life of obligations. So I lived in Berlin for a few amazing months, street performing and writing and otherwise enjoying myself immensely (in a city, I might add, where I am fully legal as an eighteen-year-old). It was awesome.

Well, perhaps most importantly, I learned, at a time when I really needed to, that I am in complete control of my life; that choosing to live an adventure was all it took, and believing in it, no matter how insane or how simple; and that I can do it my whole life. And I met so many people who were living such interesting lives, so different from anyone I'd gone to school with or known in California, even in the Bay Area. I glimpsed and got to touch and taste a way to live I'd never experienced, even for an open-minded girl in another first-world country. I wasn't staying in nice hostels and going to plays or tourist attractions; I was living in an REI sleeping bag in a bomb crater behind a squat taken over by artists. I took a risk. I left my reality and decided to believe that another was possible, and I had the time of my life.

The ease of communicating through the Internet—both to research travel options here and abroad and to keep in touch with friends and family once you're on the road—has helped take a lot of the mystery and anxiety out of venturing away from home. To educate yourself on the countries or regions you plan on visiting, you can rely on online resources and on tried-and-true, budget-minded travel guidebooks. Whenever possible, try to sit down in front of a map with someone who's been to the places you're going to go to find out what tourist sights, restaurants, and hotels they'd recommend and which ones they'd advise you to skip. It can be helpful to make and confirm any hotel and hostel reservations before you leave home, so you have an address to head to when you arrive in a new town.

FOR MORE ON TRAVEL GUIDES, SEE P. 163.

TRAVELING SAFELY

When you arrive at your destination, ask a knowledgeable and trustworthy local (such as a hotel or hostel clerk) what areas are best avoided—during the day and especially at night. If you're traveling alone, it's a good idea to walk purposefully and look like you know where you're going—even when you don't. So if you do get lost, don't stand on a busy street corner squinting and frowning over your map—a move that practically screams "easy mark" to thieves and other con artists. Instead, duck into a café as you reorient yourself.

While it's definitely unfair, female travelers need to be aware of the additional risks they face because of their gender. People in certain parts of the world believe that American women are sexually immodest, so it's important for you to understand these cultural stereotypes and do what you can to avoid situations where you might be harassed while you're traveling. In some places where custom or religious tradition dictates that women wear long skirts or scarves, you may feel strange adopting the local mode of dress. But that's one way to show respect for the people of the country you're visiting—and avoid unwanted attention.

WHAT TO PACK FOR YOUR TRIP

Here are some travel essentials that had better make their way into your suitcase!

One very comfortable pair of walking shoes

One pair of shower sandals (to avoid catching anything inconvenient in communal hostel showers)

At least three pairs of socks

At least five pairs of underwear

Gentle detergent for hand-washing clothes

A first-aid kit

A swimsuit

Sun protection: a sun hat, sunglasses, and sunscreen

A raincoat

A sewing kit

Tampons

Condoms (if you think there's a chance you may be having sex)

Any medications you take

A journal

My friend Amy and I always wanted to go travel to different places around the world, so during high school, we saved money from our part-time jobs and went around the world.

I backpacked through Europe with my best friend, my mother. I got to see different cultures and the food was awesome.

I had been saving money since I was six. With that money I went to London along with some friends, and then went on to Heidelberg, Germany, and finally to Florence, Italy. At each of these cities we established a "home base" at a youth hostel or the home of a friend. We would then take trips to places anywhere from forty miles to two countries away, for a day to even a month and a half!

I loved the experience of seeing places that had existed for thousands of years. The history was overwhelming. Also the opportunity of discovering other world views . . . I am really glad I had my friends with me. There were seven of us, and though not all of them were with us the entire time, I felt as though I had reached a new level in my relationship with each of them.

I am now in college. It was hard when I first came back to "sit still" and not travel. I also struggled when I realized how many things we daily take for granted as American citizens, as well as how ignorant many people are of the world and its problems .

Don't leave home without...

Here are some essential logistical aids and services every traveler should know about.

1. **THE INTERNATIONAL STUDENT IDENTITY CARD.**
Issued by STA Travel (http://www.statravel.com), the ISIC entitles any student or recent college graduate (up to age twenty-six) to receive discounts on everything from plane and train tickets to museums to hotel rooms. The card costs $22 and is valid for twelve months (enabling students to travel and receive its benefits even after they graduate from high school or college, so long as they enrolled while they were still in school). Card holders automatically receive basic medical insurance coverage while they're abroad, and they're entitled to contact a toll-free, twenty-four-hour help line, whose multilingual staff offers emergency financial, medical, and legal assistance to travelers.

2. **INTERNATIONAL YOUTH TRAVEL CARD.** Available to nonstudents (or part-time students), the IYTC entitles cardholders to the same insurance and travel-assistance benefits and many of the same airfare and other travel discounts as the International Student Identity Card. Valid for one year, the IYTC costs $22 and is also available through STA Travel.

3. **YOUTH HOSTEL CARD.** To stay in any one of the more than four thousand hostels affiliated with Hostelling International in sixty countries, you'll need to show a membership card. Sign up for your one-year membership for $28 through STA or Hostelling International USA. (http://www.hiayh.org).

I had saved a lot of money throughout my high school years, but I didn't know what I was going to do with it until a month after graduation. I traveled to places I always wanted to go. I went to South America and kinda backpacked from Chile to Mexico, staying a long time in Brazil.

I went to university, but had a nervous breakdown after three months. So I spent the rest of that year traveling. I loved the traveling. I loved meeting people. I loved recovering and getting better in my own way. I loved seeing the world and living on my own, seeing what I could do.

After high school, I spent four months in Tibet studying their ancient religion with my great aunt. Of course I couldn't speak the language, so I had to hire a full-time translator!

I backpacked around Europe, staying at relatives' houses in England in between going to France, Italy, Greece, Russia, Belgium, and the like. I learned some new languages and it helped open my eyes about the rest of the world before going to college.

I hated the snobbiness toward Americans. Don't they realize that we're people, too? Just because I haven't mastered the language doesn't mean that I'm to be mocked.

GENERAL SAFETY TIPS FOR WOMEN TRAVELERS

Many of the things you'll need to be mindful of while traveling alone as a woman are the same as the ones you worry about at home:

1. **Be cautious with strangers, especially male ones.**

2. **Stay in populated, brightly lit places whenever possible.**

3. **Observe (or at least be aware of) local customs and attitudes about women.**

Volunteering

If you want to do something good for the world, volunteering for a national or international organization with a well-established service program could be a great adventure for you. The best nonprofit or humanitarian programs offer structure, assistance with travel planning, and plenty of orientation, so you understand the people you'll be living among and how best to help them or the land they inhabit.

You're probably familiar with the Peace Corps, the US government's famous international volunteer program, which was founded by President John F. Kennedy in 1961. The Peace Corps almost exclusively takes volunteers who already have college degrees (and, increasingly, selects applicants with years of work experience). But there are many private and publicly run programs for younger people based in the United States and abroad that operate similarly to the Peace Corps, sending volunteers to far-flung areas in need to work in education, community development, health, disaster relief, and environmental protection. They're a great way to learn new skills and develop responsibility, and also to take on important work with tangible benefits that will last long after you've left.

US VOLUNTEER PROGRAMS

FOR NATIONAL VOLUNTEER ORGANIZATIONS, SEE P. 164.

In the United States, there are many secular and nonsecular local and national volunteer programs that actively seek young, energetic people willing to roll up their sleeves to help people less fortunate than themselves, or to work protecting vital wildlands. The biggest multipurpose national service volunteer program for young Americans is AmeriCorps, which was created in 1994 by President Bill Clinton. Following the Peace Corps model, AmeriCorps enlists fifty thousand people aged seventeen and up each year to participate in a wide range of service projects. As an umbrella organization, AmeriCorps puts its members to work around the country in more than 2,100 local nonprofit agencies, community centers, and places of worship, including the American Red Cross, Habitat for Humanity, and Boys and Girls Clubs. Members serve full- or part-time for ten months to a year, and in addition to receiving health insurance, job training, and student loan deferment, full-time members receive an education award of around $5,000 to pay for college or graduate school or pay back student loans. About half the members also receive a modest stipend for living expenses during the time of their service.

AmeriCorps has three separate wings: AmeriCorps State/National, which operates hands-on programs, such as tutoring or planting a community garden, in every state (the Web site has state-by-state listings of all affiliated nonprofit agencies currently looking for volunteers); AmeriCorps VISTA (Volunteers in Service to America), which concentrates on behind-the-scenes projects, such as setting up tutoring programs and health clinics; and AmeriCorps NCCC (National Civilian Community Corps), which runs intensive ten-month programs for eighteen- to twenty-four-year-olds on five separate campuses around the country. Typically, NCCC volunteers perform a variety of service work in disaster relief, public safety, education, and environmental projects.

INTERNATIONAL VOLUNTEER PROGRAMS

If you belong to a specific religious group, or even if you don't, chances are very good that a church or other religious organization in your community can help put you in touch with that faith's international volunteering wing. In times of political and economic hardship, governments are less likely to sponsor international aid programs, and religious groups often pick up the slack. Right now, many developing nations in Africa, Asia, and Latin America benefit greatly from the education and health programs set up and run by Jewish, Catholic, and Lutheran organizations (to name just a few) and their hardworking foreign volunteers.

Though some religious groups prefer adults with job experience to volunteer abroad, others frequently assign young people to remote posts to help teach or work on projects like building schools and hospitals, and you might very well find an exciting, unique volunteer opportunity halfway across the world by knocking on the door of a religious group in your hometown. Since some religions emphasize proselytizing—singing the praises of their faith in order to win converts—you should, however, try to find out up front if the faith-based organization you're considering volunteering with takes a secular or nonsecular approach to its service projects, and make sure that you're comfortable with the program.

Studying Abroad

If you are in college and want to study abroad, you're in luck: The easiest way to begin researching options is to take a walk across campus to your school's foreign study office. There, you should be able to learn about a wide range of programs hosted by your school or others. Typically, college students study for one or two semesters in their junior year (hence the familiar phrase "junior year abroad"), but it's also not uncommon for students to study abroad for part of their sophomore or senior year. If you happen to be majoring in a foreign language or a specific area of international history, be sure also to ask the head of your program about study-abroad programs that he or she would particularly recommend—there may well be an international language or cultural program that would fit nicely with your course of study.

If you're not yet a college student (or if you happen to suddenly develop an urge to study abroad at age sixty-eight), you may have to dig a bit more to find a study-abroad program you like, but have faith—there are literally thousands out there for travelers of all ages, emphasizing everything from fashion design to foreign language to archaeology.

I spent a year in Israel on a study-abroad program for overseas students. I had an amazing time. I loved being on my own in a different culture and meeting other kids from the country and from all over America.

My parents were worried because I went to Israel right when all the trouble was just starting, so they kept calling me, making sure I was OK anytime a bomb went off anywhere.

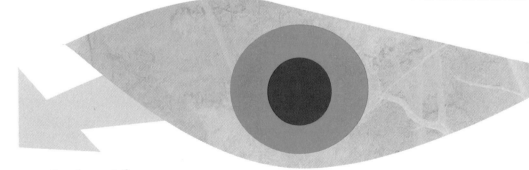

Two things to look out for:

1. Will all your credits from a foreign program transfer to your home school? Make sure you completely understand how they will transfer—before you select a school.

2. Just like college programs, certain study abroad programs offer scholarships or financial aid. Also, your home school most likely offers a certain amount of money each year.

Working Abroad

Considering the complexity of visa restrictions and the difficulty of finding a job overseas, by yourself (and without a college degree), one of the best ways to find work abroad straight out of high school (or during or shortly after college) is to sign up with one of several agencies that run international employment programs. The bartending, restaurant, and secretarial work these agencies typically put you in touch with (for a small fee) may not be in line with your ultimate career goals, but the gigs are temporary (lasting three to six months) and the chance to earn your keep while you live in a foreign country will definitely be fascinating. Having the agencies take care of your paperwork is just the icing on the cake.

Another great way for young people to see the world while earning money is to teach English in a foreign country. Some teaching programs require their instructors to have prior experience, but some (especially in countries where the demand to learn English is growing by leaps and bounds) have looser requirements. Depending on the situation, you might be assigned to teach your own classes, or assist already established teachers with their classes. Other organizations, like YMCA International (www.ymcainternational.org) offer students the chance to be camp counselors in other countries for a season.

I have a teaching "assistantship" through the French Embassy. I was assigned to a French high school just outside of Paris.

The hardest thing to deal with is the French "system"—communication with the teachers isn't always as easy as it is at home, paperwork takes longer, and it took me a month and a half to get paid (and in a city like Paris, that makes life more difficult).

FOR INFO ON TEACHING PROGRAMS SEE P. 165.
FOR IDEAS FOR FINANCING YOUR TRIP SEE P. 173.

I traveled with a carnival. It was the kind that did stuff like 4-H fairs and fall festivals. I worked the ring toss game. Ring any bottles, you won a rabbit. Ring any of the four gray bottles, you won a pygmy goat.

I got to travel and live out of a tent. Knowing I was going to be in a new town every week was a thrill.

About a month after I graduated, I packed my bags and went to Europe. I was there for about seven months. Through some family friends I got a small apartment in Finland and got a job in a clothing store. It was hard at first because not everyone speaks English, but I picked up the language pretty quickly.

I was offered a job by some relatives in Germany as a full-time nanny. I had a hard time at first, but being surrounded by German forces you to pick it up. The good part is definitely the experience of a different culture.

I have been looking for a job in India as an actress. My parents paid for acting lessons for eight years. I feel I should put my skills to work in Bollywood! Of course, I plan to keep traveling!

RESOURCES

Many of the following resources address more than one type of travel (i.e., study abroad, volunteering overseas, etc.)

Travel

National and International Organizations

The Council on International Educational Exchange offers a wide range of volunteer, teaching, work, and study programs abroad; scholarships for travel; and helpful, frequently updated travel tips.
Adddress: 7 Custom House Street, 3rd Floor, Portland, ME 04101
Phone: 800-40-STUDY
Web site: http://www.ciee.org

Hostelling International - USA, a membership organization, provides contact information for more than four thousand hostels in more than sixty countries and enables members to make and pay for reservations before leaving home.
Adddress: 8401 Colesville Road, Suite 600, Silver Spring, MD 20910
Phone: 301-495-1240
Web site: http://www.hiayh.org

Rotary International offers homestay and student exchange opportunities around the world, as well as grants and scholarships for service-minded travel programs.
Adddress: One Rotary Center, 1560 Sherman Avenue, Evanston, IL 60201
Phone: 847-866-3000
Web site: http://www.rotary.org

SERVAS, founded in 1949, is an organization designed to promote peace and put its traveler members in touch with host families around the world who are willing to put them up for two- and three-night stays. The room and board is free, but the idea is for travelers to stay long enough with their host families to forge a connection.
Adddress: United States SERVAS, 11 John Street, Room 505, New York, NY 10038
Phone: 212-267-0252
Web site: http://www.usservas.org

Books

The Back Door Guide to Short-Term Job Adventures by Michael Landes (Ten Speed Press). A comprehensive source of information about internships, seasonal work, volunteer opportunities, and overseas jobs.

The Directory of Websites for International Jobs by Ron and Caryl Krannich (Impact Publications). Lists more than 1,400 Web sites that can help expats find jobs in for-profit and nonprofit sectors and contact each other.

The High School Student's Guide to Study, Travel, and Adventure Abroad (CIEE). An invaluable introduction to more than two hundred international educational volunteering, homestay, and travel programs.

A Journey of One's Own by Thalia Zepatos (Eight Mountain Press) offers advice and encouragement to women looking to travel solo.

The **Let's Go** series of country-by-country guidebooks (Let's Go Travel Publications) are written by and for students and loaded with budget-minded travel information.

The **On a Shoestring** series of guidebooks (Lonely Planet Publications), covering wide regions such as Southeast Asia and West Africa, are the well-researched, well-thumbed backpack bibles of many young travelers.

Safety and Security for Women Who Travel, by Peter Laufer and Sheila Swan (Travelers' Tales) is packed with common-sense advice and safety suggestions on how to avoid and deal with trouble on the road.

Taking Time Off by Colin Hall and Ron Lieber (Noonday Press). A *New York Times* bestseller, this lively guide shares the stories of students who took successful breaks from college and offers advice on how to plan one of your own.

Tales of a Female Nomad by Rita Gelman (Three Rivers Press) describes the author's adventures with places and people all over the world.

Web sites

The Center for Interim Programs at http://interimprograms.com has been arranging travel, study, and volunteer breaks for college students and adults since 1980. For a fee of $1,900, the Center will assess your interests and goals and put you in touch with any of three thousand different programs.

The Centers for Disease Control at http://www.cdc.gov/travel/ offers up-to-the-minute information on health alerts and immunization requirements for all countries.

Learning through Experience at http://www.learn4you.com/home.html helps college-age students find alternative national and international internship, apprenticeship, and field-study programs for a fee.

The US Department of State at http://www.state.gov/travel/ is a comprehensive gateway to useful information on traveler safety and visa requirements, as well as specific travel tips for students and women.

www.whereyouheaded.com offers time-off consulting online for a flat fee of $50.

Volunteering

National and International Organizations

The American Jewish Society for Service runs programs in forty-five states, sponsoring projects such as building schools and community centers and installing water systems in impoverished areas.
Address: 15 East 26th Street, Room 1029, New York, NY 10010.
Phone: 212-683-6178
Web site: http://www.ajss.org

AmeriCorps
Address: 1201 New York Avenue, NW, Washington, DC 20525
Phone: 800-942-2677
Website: http://www.americorps.org

The National Park Service offers volunteers a wide range of opportunities in such locations as the Appalachian National Scenic Trail and Yosemite National Park.
Address: 1849 C Street NW, Washington, DC 20240
Phone: 202-208-6843
Web site: http://www.nps.gov/volunteer

The **Student Conservation Association** works in conjunction with national and state parks, placing teams of students all over the country to assist with different park programs, from trail building to backcountry patrolling.
Address: 689 River Road, PO Box 550, Charlestown, NH 03603
Phone: 603-543-1700
Web site: http://www.thesca.org

Books

The International Directory of Voluntary Work (Peterson's) contains information on seven hundred organizations in need of short- and long-term volunteers with varied skills.

Summer Jobs for Students (Peterson's). A guide to more than twenty-five thousand summer jobs in the US and Canada, including many volunteer positions with national parks and arts organizations.

Web sites

Amigos de las Americas, at www.amigoslink.org, is a volunteer service organization that has sponsored public health projects in Mexico, the Caribbean, and Central and South America since 1965.

Green Volunteers at http://www.greenvol.com is an information network for international voluntary work in nature conservation.

Idealist.org at http://idealist.org is a consortium of over thirty-five thousand nonprofit and community organizations in 165 countries, which you can search or browse by name, location, or mission to find volunteer opportunities around the world.

Volunteers for Peace, at http://www.vfp.org, founded in 1981, coordinates a wide variety of volunteer work camps throughout the US, Europe, North Africa, Central America, and the countries of the former Soviet Union.

World-Wide Opportunities in Organic Farming at http://www.wwoof.org is a nonprofit homestay program that hooks volunteers eager to·learn organic farming methods up with farms in more than twenty countries.

Teaching abroad

Organizations

WorldTeach at http://www.worldteach.org runs summer English-teaching programs in Costa Rica, Equador, Namibia, and Poland for all people eighteen and older, and year-long programs in Costa Rica, Namibia, and the Marshall Islands for those with college degrees.

YMCA International runs an International Camp Counselor Program that places students in camps around the world, usually for the summer (but keep in mind that "summer" in the Southern Hemisphere is from December to February!).
Web site: http://www.ymcainternational.org

Studying abroad

Book

The Insider's Guide to Study Abroad by Ann M. Moore (Peterson's Guides). Written by the director of study-abroad programs at the College of William and Mary, this detailed book offers the lowdown on visas, financial planning, credit transfers, and culture shock.

financing
your dream

While some people are lucky enough to have parents or other relatives pay for college or another type of schooling after high school, or even sponsor travel or struggling artists' careers, many people have to find outside sources of funding for these expensive endeavors. Fortunately, there are a number of ways you can corral enough cash to further your education (whatever form it takes), to supplement the amount of money that your family can contribute, or to cover your costs in full. About half of all college students receive grant aid from at least one source. According to the New York Times, in 2003 financial aid in the form of grants and loans totaled more than $105 billion.

When you are trying to figure out what your costs will be, remember to include:

Tuition and school fees

Room and board

Books and supplies

Computer supplies and software

Fees for any extracurricular activities (sororities, etc.)

Personal expenses (laundry, phone, social outings, etc.)

Travel (especially high if you live out of state)

Financial Aid for College and Other Post-secondary Schooling

Since higher education is a great opportunity for you to enrich yourself, you and your parents should carefully consider all the costs involved and to what extent these costs will put you and/or your family in debt after you're finished. There may be some financial responsibilities you'd willingly accept in order to pursue certain academic goals, and others you'd rather not. But always bear in mind that you don't necessarily have to have a lot of money in order to attend your first-choice college or earn your dream degree, since financial aid for higher education and other forms of financial assistance are specifically designed to help people achieve these goals. Before you start to research, try to get a clear sense of what your financial needs will be, including all living expenses and school fees.

"Financial aid" is the term used to describe all kinds of monetary assistance available to help students attend two- and four-year colleges and other kinds of accredited post-secondary vocational or technical schools. It's available from federal and state governments, institutions, and other private sources, and it generally consists of loans (which must be paid back), work (employment opportunities that give students a chance to earn money to help cover their education costs), and scholarships and grants (which do not have to be paid back). Students who qualify for financial aid may receive assistance from one source or from a combination of sources. About half of all college students receive financial aid in one form or another.

Most financial aid is known as "need-based," since it's awarded based on an individual's degree of financial need. The other major kind of financial aid is known as "merit-based," since it's typically awarded to students who have a certain grade point average or who display special skills and talents in areas such as athletics or the performing arts.

In most cases, students and their parents are both expected to help pay for college expenses, and the amount of need-based financial aid you qualify for is determined by subtracting the amount you and your parents can contribute from the cost of attending a given college or technical school. The amount you and your family can pay—your so-called expected family contribution—is determined by your family's income, size, and whether other members are also enrolled in college, among other factors.

There are some circumstances, however, in which students are considered legally independent of their parents: if they're married, over age twenty-four, veterans of the US armed forces, or able to document extraordinary circumstances with the financial aid offices of the schools they'd like to attend. If you happen to fall into any one of these categories, your financial information will be considered on its own—unless you're married, in which case your spouse's financial information will also have to be supplied on your application for financial aid.

FEDERAL FINANCIAL AID

The primary source of assistance for students attending secondary school, federal financial aid, comes in two forms: aid for students and aid for parents. To qualify, students must be citizens of the US (or eligible noncitizens), be enrolled in or accepted to an eligible institution, be in good academic standing, and not be in default of any previous financial aid received from any institution.

FAFSA

The standard procedure for applying for federal financial aid is to complete and submit the Free Application for Federal Student Aid (FAFSA), on which you'll be asked to document all your financial details, along with any other financial aid applications required by the individual school or schools you'd like to attend. But since different schools have different procedures for submitting the FAFSA (and any other applications they require), you should always check first with the financial aid office of the schools you're applying to in order to find out what specific steps you'll need to take.

In most cases, FAFSA forms (available at www.fafsa.ed.gov) are due between January 1 and February 15. However, students are generally advised to submit the forms as soon as they can after January 1 to make sure they meet all state aid deadlines and have enough time to correct any mistakes on the form. About two weeks after you submit your FAFSA forms, you should receive back a preliminary student aid report on which you may be required to make certain corrections. And about two or three weeks after that, you should get back a final report with a calculation of your expected family contribution—the amount of money you and your parents will be expected to pay.

Below, you'll find a rundown of the most widely used forms of federal aid. But first, two words of advice: Since guidelines are subject to change, be sure you check the US Department of Education for the latest detailed information on all forms of government aid to students. And, since not every school participates in every available financial aid program, be sure to check in early with the financial aid offices of the schools where you're applying to find out which programs they do participate in.

> I have federal loans and I am also in a program where my permanent address is out-of-state but because of my major, I receive in-state tuition.
> (Middle Tennessee State University, Murfreesboro)

> By filling out the FAFSA, I received my state and federal aid. They even gave me a check for the remainder of the money I received. It's awesome. I get paid to go to school. They also pay for my books.
> (Hudson Valley Community College, Troy, NY)

Grants

Pell grants are need-based grants available to undergraduates, which do not have to be repaid. The amount of a student's Pell grant depends on several factors, including expected contributions from family, the structure and length of a program of study, and whether the student is attending school full- or part-time.

Federal Supplemental Educational Grants (FSEOG) are need-based awards available to undergraduates with exceptional financial need.

SEE P. 177 FOR STUDENT AID RESOURCES.

Loans

Borrowing money is a very scary thing and there are many factors to consider, especially if you are faced with having to turn down a college because no other financial sources have appeared. It can be especially helpful to talk to other adults who have taken out loans to better understand the long-term impact of this choice. It may be that you are going into a career with a very high earning potential and you feel a loan is a gamble you can afford to take, or you might be totally unsure, which can make taking on the commitment even harder.

There are many different kinds of education loans. Before taking out any loan, be sure to ask the following kinds of questions:

>> **How much do you really need?**

>> Are you paying back the loan all by yourself or with help from your parents?

>> **What is the interest rate of the loan?**

>> Exactly how much has to be paid in interest?

>> **What will the monthly payments be?**

>> How many years will you be paying back the loans?

>> **When do you have to start paying back the loan?**

>> Are there certain times/circumstances in your life when you will be able to stop making payments?

The answers to these questions can help you get a better handle on what taking out a loan can mean to you down the road.

> Collegeboard.com has a very useful college loan calculator at http://apps.collegeboard.com/fincalc/sla.html.

The Federal Perkins Loan program offers low-interest loans to under-graduate or graduate students with the greatest need. Students who borrow money through the Perkins program aren't required to make any loan payments until nine months after they graduate.

Subsidized Stafford or Direct Loans are both low-interest, need-based loan programs sponsored by the federal government. The federal government pays the interest for you while you're in school (that's why they're called "subsidized"), and you become responsible for making the interest payments six months after you graduate.

HOW I GOT HERE

If Jimmy Carter hadn't been President when it was time for me to go to college, I couldn't have gone at all. There were easy ways for kids with no money or parental support to go to school then. So he's a hero to me. Seriously, I love Jimmy Carter.

—LYNDA BARRY, CARTOONIST

I receive the Millennium Scholarship. It is offered to students in my state who graduate high school with a GPA of 3.5 or higher. I am so grateful for this scholarship. (University of Las Vegas, NV)

I received financial aid and a scholarship. I asked my parents if their jobs offered scholarships for employees' kids. Ask to see if either parent was a vet in any major war; that helps in getting scholarships. And do lots of web searches. (Michigan State University, East Lansing)

Federal Unsubsidized Stafford or Direct Loans are for students who do not demonstrate financial need but, for a variety of reasons, require extra money to help cover school costs. Recipients of unsubsidized Stafford loans must pay interest while they're in school, or, alternatively, they can wait and begin paying the accrued interest—on top of the balance of the loan—up to six months after finishing school. (Though many choose to delay paying interest until after graduation, the disadvantage of deferring interest payments is that they accrue on top of the amount of the loan, forcing you to pay more money to the lender over time.)

Federal Parent Loans for Undergraduate Students (a program also known as PLUS) is the largest source of parent loans. Under this program, parents of dependent children can borrow up to the cost of attendance minus any other financial aid received by the student.

Work

Federal Work-Study (FWS) provides jobs—typically in school libraries, cafeterias, or athletic facilities—for students eligible for financial aid. It gives students the chance to earn money to help defray the cost of their education.

I receive a scholarship from Veterans Affairs. It allows me to have free tuition to any college in California. I received this because my dad served in the navy.
(San Diego State University, CA)

I received an academic scholarship, a music scholarship, and federal student loans.
(Central College, Pella, IA)

Tap into the Scholarship Gold Mine

Since many towns, states, employers, and local organizations (such as religious groups and the Rotary and Lions Clubs) donate money to college students on a regular basis, the best place to look for scholarship money might well be in your own backyard. Here are some creative strategies—and important questions to ask—to track down cash for college in your hometown.

1. Many companies offer scholarships for employees' children, so ask your parents to inquire about this with the personnel departments at their jobs.

2. If you have a job yourself, ask your boss if the company you work for has any scholarship funds.

3. Find out if a church or synagogue in your town offers a scholarship program—whether or not you're a member, you may be able to apply.

4. Ask your high school guidance counselor if your school offers any scholarships for students who excel in various subjects or extracurriculars.

5. Find out if any of the clubs or organizations you're involved with—athletic, artistic, academic, or otherwise—provide scholarships to members. (Also, ask your parents to find out if the organizations they're involved with offer scholarships for members' children.)

6. Type the word "scholarship" into your local newspaper's online archive and see what comes up—normally, scholarships are publicly announced in the spring, so you can limit the time frame of your search from, say, March to June, to hone in on mentions of scholarships awarded in your area.

STATE FINANCIAL AID

State financial aid comes in variety of forms. Some states offer financial aid to state residents who attend school in-state; some states offer aid to students who attend school in-state or out-of-state; and some offer aid to students who attend school in their state even if they reside in another. Contact your state scholarship office and the financial aid office of any specific school you'd like to attend to find out what kind of state aid may be available to you.

PRIVATE (A.K.A. ALTERNATIVE) FINANCIAL AID

While it's always a good idea to pursue federal financial aid first, since the loans offered under government programs are the least expensive and most flexible, you may also want to consider taking out a loan with one of the many private institutions that lend money to students. Many alternative loan programs offer the options of deferring payment on the principal (the total amount you borrow to pay for school) or deferring payment on the interest until after you graduate. But it's a good idea, if at all possible, to start making interest payments while you're in school, so the interest doesn't get added onto the principle—making the total amount you'd owe after school that much greater.

SCHOLARSHIPS

Though the famous full-scholarship "free ride" to college is, alas, a rarity, there are thousands of different scholarship programs in the United States just waiting to hand out grants of various sizes to students who can demonstrate economic need or special aptitudes and talents. Finding scholarships tailor-made for you can take a bit of digging, but your guidance counselor, local library, and state scholarship office should be able to give you some good ideas about where to look.

I have both a music scholarship and an academic scholarship. I auditioned for the music one and the academic one was based on my grades from high school.

(College of Wooster, OH)

SURPRISING SCHOLARSHIPS

Duck Brand Duct Tape Stuck at Prom Contest
Grandma Scholarship
Little People of America Award
National Make it Yourself with Wool Scholarship
Klingon Language Institute Scholarship
Patrick Kerr Skateboard Scholarship
Tupperware Home Parties Scholarship
Chick and Sophie Major Memorial Duck Calling Contest
All-American Apple Pie Recipe Contest

Financing Your Travel

If you can't rely on your parents for help, there are many other ways to find funding for your trip. Though many volunteer programs will provide you with room and board for the length of your stay, most require you to pay your own travel expenses to get to and from your destination. And naturally, study courses all require tuition. But don't let that hold you back.

ALSO SEE P. 139 FOR IDEAS FOR HIGH-PAYING SHORT-TERM WORK.

Maybe you can live at home and work hard for half a year to raise enough money to travel for the next six months. Or maybe you can approach your school or community groups (such as the Lions Club, Rotary Club, Kiwanis Club, or your local chamber of commerce) about making a contribution, in exchange for which you might offer to make a video presentation or give a talk about your experience when you return.

If you plan to volunteer overseas, you may want to appeal to civic-minded neighborhood associations or church groups who will be impressed by your desire to help others. Enlisting friends for a bake sale or car wash is another good way to go. And if you intend to travel independently, try putting fliers on local bulletin boards to find work cutting lawns, babysitting, or walking dogs as a way of raising cash.

You may also be eligible for a travel grant. Some colleges offer scholarships to students studying abroad; check with your school's financial aid office to see if there are any available at your school. The Council on International Educational Exchange offers several different grants and scholarships to students participating in any one of its educational, work, voluntary service, or internship programs. Many volunteer programs also offer financial assistance to applicants who need it; be sure to find out if yours does, and apply for it if you qualify.

FOR MORE IDEAS ON HOW OTHER GIRLS HAVE FINANCED THEIR TRIPS, SEE P. 162.

Managing Your Money

For many people, graduating from high school means managing a significant amount of money for the very first time. Whether you're heading to college, entering the world of work, or preparing to travel for awhile, you need to learn how to create a budget to cover your monthly expenses, set aside money for emergencies, and develop a certain amount of discipline where spending is concerned. Temptations to drop a few bucks are every-where—new jeans, shoes, music, movies, a quick road trip—and recent high school graduates who aren't used to financial discipline often run into debt that can take them years to pay off. So, while it may not be the most exciting aspect of becoming an adult, it's very important to be responsible about money and establish spending and saving patterns now that will serve you well now and in the future.

SETTING UP A CHECKING ACCOUNT

If you're going to be managing your own money, you'll need to set up a checking account, or checking and savings accounts, at a bank near your school or place of work. This will allow you to keep your paychecks, college loan money, and/or allowances from parents in a safe, convenient place and provide you with blank checks and an ATM card (or an ATM/debit card) to cover your expenses. With a standard ATM card, you can make deposits and withdrawals and conduct other transactions at ATM machines managed by your local bank, twenty-four hours a day, without charge. And with an ATM/debit card, you can use your card at stores to make purchases that will be automatically deducted from the balance in your checking account.

The school you're attending or your employer can probably steer you to a bank in the area that has a good record of customer service. If your school or company has a business relationship with this particular bank, it may be able to provide you with a letter of introduction to the bank that will make it possible for you to open an account with even a very minimal amount of money to start. Every bank has different requirements for setting up a checking account. Some require a minimum average monthly balance if you want to avoid service fees; some offer free checking, and some offer accounts specially designed for students that typically require a lower minimum balance to avoid fees. So be sure to read the fine print as you're researching banks and their various types of accounts: Your goal is to find a place that will charge you no service fees, or only very low ones, for the types of transactions you're likely to be making.

BALANCING YOUR CHECKING ACCOUNT

Writing down the date, direction (i.e., deposit or withdrawal), and purpose (e.g., a debit withdrawal for groceries, a deposit of your weekly paycheck, or a check you wrote to your school's bookstore to pay for new textbooks) of all your financial transactions is the cleanest, easiest way to keep track of exactly how much money you have in your account. If you don't carry your checkbook with you every day, save all receipts from ATM and debit purchases in your wallet, then sit down once a week (or so) and enter them into your checkbook ledger. This way, you'll have a single, up-to-date record of your account balance in your ledger, and you'll drastically reduce the risk of overdrawing—writing a check you don't have enough money to cover. You may also be able to get online access to your checking account, which will allow you to monitor all your transactions. Many banks offer auto-pay features that you can use to be sure you never forget to pay a bill on time.

Number	Date	Description of Transaction	Payment/Debit		Deposit/Credit		BALANCE $2130	32
171	9/1/3	DUKE UNIVERSITY BOOKSTORE	72	95			72	95
		(INTRO TO PSYCH TEXTBOOK)					2057	37
	9/4/3	ATM WITHDRAWAL (COFFEE, SNACKS, MOVIE)	40	00			40	00
							2017	37
	9/10/3	BIRTHDAY CHECK FROM GRANDMA			150	00	150	00
							2167	37

DESIGNING AND STICKING TO A BUDGET

Another important reason to keep a detailed, up-to-date account of transactions in your ledger is that this record will allow you to see exactly where you're spending your money—and where you may need to rein in some expenditures in order to live within your means.

The first step in determining a budget is to figure out how much money you have to spend every month. If you've got a relatively large check from a student loan sitting in your account at the beginning of a semester, for example, divide that amount by the number of months the money needs to last; the amount you come up with is your monthly allowance. If you're beginning a new job, the total of your monthly paychecks is the amount of money you now have to spend every month.

Once you've figured out your monthly allowance, you need to subcategorize, figuring out what amount you will spend on food and housing (including utility bills, such as phone and electric), transportation, clothing, and entertainment. The first item in that list of expenditures is truly necessary, and the last one is, arguably, expendable. Only you can decide how you want to spend your money—where you want to economize and where you want to splurge now and then. But the point is to establish a regular spending pattern that does not exceed what you can actually pay for. People who write checks with insufficient funds in their accounts—

forcing their checks to "bounce"—are charged penalties in the neighborhood of $30 by their banks every time this happens and sometimes fined even more by the place where they wrote the check that bounced. In the end, living within your budget will save you from innumerable hassles—and ever-mounting expenses.

CREDIT CARDS

Credit-card commercials on TV typically show well-dressed, smiling couples using credit cards to pay for lavish dinners, and it's no accident that these ads leave many people with the impression that pulling out the plastic is a fast and easy path to the lush life. But in reality, credit cards often cause financial problems that can take years—if not decades—for people to resolve.

Credit-card companies want people to use their cards regularly, and they want people to spend a lot—more than they can actually pay off when the bill comes due—because that's how they make their money. Credit-card holders are required to make a minimum monthly payment, and then the credit-card company can charge interest—sometimes more than 20 percent—on the remaining amount owed. So if you're carrying credit-card debt of $1000 for an extended period of time—essentially, a loan from the credit-card company—that means you could be required to pay $200 or more in interest charges in a year.

To be sure, there are advantages to using credit cards. They offer a secure, convenient way of paying for online or catalogue purchases, and in many places people can't rent cars or hotel rooms or purchase plane tickets without them. They're also extremely helpful when you really do need a short-term loan to cover medical or other expenses in emergency situations. And by using a credit card and making substantial payments to reduce your balance regularly (and, ideally, paying off your balance in full every month, to avoid interest), you can establish a record of good credit that will help you if and when you approach a bank in the future, seeking a home mortgage or car loan. (If your credit history shows that you've been a responsible borrower over the years, you're more likely to be granted the loan.)

Still, it's extremely important to recognize the danger of racking up overwhelming credit-card debt, because it has a funny way of mounting fast. In an effort to get people to use their credit cards more, companies regularly increase the total amount that long-time cardholders can charge. And to woo new customers, lending companies actively seek out recent high school graduates to get them to sign up for their first cards.

(Passing out T-shirts and Frisbees on college campuses is just one attention-grabbing sales technique.) But just because credit-card money is readily available—as fast as a magnetic strip can be swiped—does not mean that it's a good idea for people to spend it. College administrators say that it's not uncommon these days for students who become buried under credit-card debt to drop out before graduation. So especially for young people taking on the responsibility of managing their own finances for the first time, it is extremely important to use credit cards wisely.

RESOURCES

Books

The College Board College Cost & Financial Aid Handbook (College Board), updated annually, provides information on financial aid available at 2,700 four- and two-year colleges.

College Student's Guide to Merit and Other No-Need Funding by Gail Ann Schlachter and R. David Weber (Reference Service Press) is a no-nonsense guide to 1,100 funding programs that never take income level into account.

Scholarships, Grants, and Prizes (Peterson's Guides) is an annual bible of more than 1.5 million academic awards and prizes.

Web sites

College-Scholarships.com at http://www.college-scholarships.com can connect you to ten free scholarship search engines.

The College Board's Scholarship Search Page at http://apps.collegeboard.com/cbsearch_ss/welcome.jsp can help you locate information on scholarships, internships, grants, and loans.

Juco.com's Financial Aid Page at http://www.juco.com/resources/financial.asp provides information on scholarship and financial aid resources for students attending junior and community colleges, as well as helpful links to loan services for all kinds of post-secondary education.

FastWeb at http://www.fastweb.com offers free searches to more than 600,000 scholarships.

LoanFinder at http://apps.estudentloan.com/exec/loanfinder can help you calculate the differences between private and government loans.

The US Department of Education's Federal Student Aid Page at http://www.ed.gov/studentaid offers plainspoken help for every stage of the financial aid application process.

CitiAssist at http://www.citiassist.com, a division of CitiBank, offers deferred-principal and/or deferred-interest loans to students.

Sallie Mae at http://salliemae.com is the biggest provider of private educational loans in the US.

Making the most

After high school comes the first step of the next phase of your life. You are leaving a controlled, familiar environment for a self-determined new experience—whether it's college, some other form of education, work, or travel. Along the way, you will meet new people, develop new relationships, encounter new situations, learn new things about the world (and yourself), and grow as a person. Whatever choices you make and paths you pursue, you'll reap the greatest rewards if you approach this time actively with an open mind (and an open heart too). This is a time brimming with possibilities—take advantage of the opportunities that will undoubtedly surround you.

Sometimes change can be overwhelming. Give yourself a chance to get acclimated to your new circumstances before making any rash judgments about whether something is or isn't working. It can take time to adapt.

Whatever you do, do it fully. Focus on what you are doing to the greatest extent possible so that you really experience it and get the most out of it. Sure, you can coast through college without much studying, or traipse across Europe in a beer-glazed haze, but you will be missing more than you'll ever know, and the loss will be your own. You will only be where you are once in your life: This is your chance to gain what you can from your experiences.

people

Be open to the people who you meet during this time. Many of them, having come from different backgrounds than you, will have valuable things to teach—and you can probably learn a lot from one another. Going through new experiences together with other people often creates strong bonds that can last a lifetime. You never know which people in your life will introduce you to exciting, new opportunities—whether educational, work-related or social.

# of your experience

learning

Take time to simply learn. Be curious. Expose yourself to as much as possible. If you are getting a formal education, remember that all your learning doesn't need to be about your major, no matter what you are studying. If you are enrolled in school, find out which departments at your college are the most highly regarded and try to take a class there simply because you can. If you have the time and resources to learn new things, do it!

Learning is a luxury. If you are at a point in your life when you have the freedom to spend time on your education, use it. If you are not in school, approach life as a learning experience. Be open to all the new things you come across in your new environment.

life experience

All experiences are valuable in some way or other—even the negative ones. As the old saying goes, experience is what you get when you don't get what you want. Even if things seem like they are going badly or you are doing something that you are not enjoying, you never know how that experience might contribute something to your life down the line. Stay open to what life after high school has to teach you—academically and otherwise.

Reach out to new people, things and experiences...

Get involved in the world.

Have fun.

Enjoy the ride!

INDEX

The award-winning gURL.com is one of the leading online sites for teenage girls. gURL has produced stories, games, interactive content and books with an independent editorial voice since 1996. gURL is an iVillage Inc property.

Check out www.gurl.com